BUILDING GOOD TEAMMATES

The Story of My Mount Rushmore, a Coaching Epiphany, and *That* Nun

LANCE LOYA

ACKNOWLEDGEMENTS

A project of this magnitude does not happen without the help of others. I am grateful to so many people, but none more so than my wife, Rachel. Her patience, sacrifice, and unwavering support are appreciated more than she will ever know. Thank you for consistently reminding me to just keep swimming.

To my daughters, Laken and Lakota, thank you for providing me with endless inspiration. I hope one day this book provides you with some insight into your dad's life and what mattered to him. May you always remember to be good teammates, and may you always have the energy to carry on this mission long after I am gone.

Thank you to Aaron Patrick. I am so proud of you and could not fathom a more deserving individual to have been honored as a recipient of the NABC Allstate Good Works Team award. You seem to never hesitate to thank me for coaching you, but the reality is that you taught me more than I ever taught you. A tip of the hat to Aaron's parents, Cliff and Michele Patrick, for raising such a fine young man and instilling in him at an early age the value of being a good teammate.

Thank you to Jack Loya, Mike Burton, Dennis Gibson, and Tim Kelly—the four men on my personal Mount Rushmore. You all impacted my life and I am appreciative of your various contributions. Of course, I could not thank you without also thanking your wives and families. They generously shared you with me and countless other impressionable players over the years. I hope Mary Loya, Di Burton, Kerry Gibson, and Joan Kelly know their own sacrifices were not in vain.

My basketball gratitude is not limited to just those four men, either. Thank you to every player who ever played for me and to every coach I ever played for. Each and every one of you touched my life and played a part in the person I have become.

I would like to recognize Cindy Davis and Craig Sikurinec for their assistance. You both graciously shared your ideas with me and provided me with valuable insight. Many thanks.

Thank you to Chris O'Byrne and everyone at JETLAUNCH Publishing. You were fantastic to work with, and your talents brought life to my epiphany. Someday maybe we will look back at this book as the start of a movement.

Finally, thank you to Sister Eric Marie Setlock for sharing so much of her wisdom with me. We spent many, many hours discussing the topics covered in this book. She is truly blessed, and so am I for having her in my life. Sister Eric Marie epitomizes what it means to be a good teammate, and continues to espouse the values Catherine McAuley envisioned for the Sisters of Mercy almost two centuries ago.

CONTENTS

INTRODUCTION

FOR as long as I can remember, the NCAA basketball tournament, a.k.a. *The Big Dance*, has been an important event in my life. I love that tournament. The excitement of the announcement of the brackets was a big deal to me as a kid. In pre-Internet days, I would sit in front of the television and painstakingly write out by hand the names and seeds of every participant in the tournament, as they were announced on the pairing show. I waited anxiously for the occasion every year.

My obsession with the tournament even caused me to get in trouble once in high school. I had asked for a hall pass to be excused from geometry class, but instead of going to the restroom, I locked myself into the television production room so that I could watch the opening round of "March Madness."

I may have gotten in trouble when I got caught that day, but the experience became a defining moment in my life. From that point on, my life's ambition was to make it into the NCAA tournament. Unfortunately, I never made it there as a player, and the closest I've gotten as a coach was watching one of my players get honored on the court for unrelated reasons during a timeout at the 2014 Final Four semifinal game.

I am as proud of that moment, however, as I imagine I would be if I had found myself coaching in the national championship. The experience of watching that player receive his special award led to me having a complete change in priorities and an epiphany of sorts—*we are emphasizing the wrong thing.*

As coaches, we teach kids how to be competitive, and there's nothing wrong with that. But in amateur sports, teaching kids to be competitive should take a backseat to teaching kids how to be good teammates, for this is a skill that will provide greater benefit to players as they transition into the real world.

With the goal of capturing the essence of my newfound belief and conveying it to a younger generation, I wrote and illustrated a children's book, aptly titled *Be a Good Teammate.* I originally intended it as a way for me to plant seeds in the impressionable minds of my own daughters and provide them with a blueprint for a happy, successful future.

The children's book blossomed into much more than I could have ever hoped. Its message resonated with people of all ages, and I suspect that is why the book was so well received. We can all learn from it, even though it is written on a very basic level.

Entailed in the pages that follow is an adult version of that book. It expands on the message and describes how the most unlikely catalyst—a nearly eighty-year-old nun—inspired me to find ways to teach players to be good teammates. This exceptionally gifted woman also got me to take a reflective look at my unusual past and see how the four men who made the biggest impact in my life—my personal Mount Rushmore—contributed to my understanding of the virtue of trust and what it means to be a good teammate.

My coaching colleagues are always asking me about *that* nun. They'll say things like: "What is the deal with *that* nun you're always talking to?" or, "Who is *that* nun with your players?" or, "Why is *that* nun speaking to your team?"

They are right to be curious. She possesses an almost magical, Mary Poppins-ish grace, and she has been a tremendous influence on both the players I coach and me.

I hope you enjoy the story of my Mount Rushmore, a coaching epiphany, and *that* nun...

1

A COACHING EPIPHANY DERIVED FROM TURBULENT TRUST

TURBULENCE. I am not sure there is a word that causes more anxiety for reluctant flyers than *turbulence*. It causes hearts to palpitate, palms to sweat, and nervous stomachs to churn. All of which oddly authenticate the apprehension associated with air travel.

Although I had flown many times before, the turbulence on this particular flight was especially rough, and it had me abnormally uneasy. As the other passengers and I bounced in our seats, enduring what seemed like a repetitive drop down the scariest part of the world's scariest roller coaster, a strange thought crossed my mind:

What if this is it?
What if this plane goes down, and this is how my life ends?

A myriad of other related questions accompanied this one, all of them racing through my head at, well, the speed of thought.

For what do I want to be remembered?
Did I accomplish enough with the time I did have?
Will I be missed?

I thought of my two pre-school aged daughters. If this plane does go down, what would I want them to know about me? What would I want to say to them before I died? This specific question struck a chord, and I became fixated on it.

What final message would I want to tell my daughters?

The obvious choice would be to simply tell them, "I love you." But as I pondered those words, they somehow did not seem to suffice. Of course I loved them. What doting father doesn't love his daughters? I suspect I had uttered that phrase to them on enough previous occasions to affirm the sentiment.

Then again, at their present age, did it even matter? As the years pass, how likely would they remember me saying those words? Would knowing that their father loved them make an impact on the future they were going to live? I needed to tell them something more. Something deeper. Something more valuable.

As the plane continued to bounce, I continued to think.

I wondered what one bit of advice could I leave with my girls that would serve them well for the rest of their lives, assuring them a future full of happiness and perhaps success?

Should it be for them to follow their dreams? To take time to smell the roses? Should I advise them to find a way to get paid to do their favorite hobby, so they will never have to truly work a day in their lives? Or maybe I should just tell them to marry someone rich and pursue a life of ease.

I started to think about how I came to be on this flight to begin with, and then the answer I was looking for suddenly presented itself.

I was heading home from Dallas, Texas, where only hours earlier I had witnessed one of the basketball players I coached accept the most prestigious award any student athlete in the history of our college had ever received. For that matter, it was arguably the most prestigious award any college athlete could receive. The player's name was Aaron Patrick, and he was just recognized on center court during the NCAA men's basketball Final Four as a recipient of the National Association of Basketball Coaches (NABC) All-state Good Works Team award.

That's a mouthful. What matters is that the award was given by the NABC, the most influential group in the sport of basketball, generously sponsored by the Allstate Insurance Company, and presented annually to a group of college basketball players who have "made a commitment to improving their communities and the lives of others."[1]

What added significance to this award is that students from our tiny school do not usually get this level of recognition. Mount Aloysius is only a small, liberal arts college situated in the very rural mountains of western Pennsylvania with an enrollment of barely a thousand students. Athletically, we compete at the NCAA Division III level. By comparison, other recipients of the Allstate Good Works Team Award included Jordan Morgan (University of Michigan), Joe Harris (University of Virginia), and Aaron Craft ("THE" Ohio State University). In the basketball world, these are household names. For everyone else, if their names aren't familiar, the names of their schools certainly are. The reality is that there were probably more students in Aaron Craft's freshman English class at Ohio State than there were in Aaron Patrick's entire graduating class at Mount Aloysius.

A panel comprised of nationally prominent coaches, former student athletes, and members of the media voted on the award. The selection committee was chaired by former Duke University All-American and seven-time NBA All-Star Grant Hill. Other members of the panel included Greg Anthony (UNLV/TNT), Seth Greenburg (ESPN), Bobby Cremins (Georgia Tech/College of Charleston), and Seth Davis (CBS/Sports Illustrated). I suspect none of them had ever even heard of Mount Aloysius College, and had no idea how to even pronounce its name. (*For the record, it is pronounced: Mount Aloe-wish-us.*)

Even now, when I sit back and look at the names above, I cannot help but come to the same conclusion as I did when I initially learned Aaron had been chosen for the award: A player from our school is not supposed to be mentioned in the same breath as *them*.

It was not some inferiority complex, either. There were volumes of statistical data supporting the fact. Aaron Patrick was not supposed to be there. And yet, he was.

Organizations like the NCAA and the NABC are always soliciting nominations for awards. Like most coaches, I try to do my due diligence and go through the motions of submitting a player's name, knowing full well that people from schools like ours never get chosen. I suppose the logic for me is to tell the players that it is an honor just to be nominated. They get something to put on their resume, and our administration gets something to brag about. To win an award of this magnitude, though, is so profound that it is almost overwhelming.

When I first received the call from Rick Leddy of the NABC notifying me that Aaron Patrick was one of the award's recipients, I thought it was a mix-up. When the realization finally set in that it was no mistake, I was euphoric. I had taken Leddy's call right before walking into practice, and my euphoria accompanied me there. Our team was coming off a tough loss to an opponent we should have beaten and preparing for a game against a perennial conference power, an opponent we were unlikely to beat. The mood was somber, with a lack of enthusiasm looming over the start of practice.

As I entered the gym, I could feel the negative vibes radiating from the players. I understood why they were feeling the way they were, but they were yet to understand why I was feeling the way I was. After observing the players for a few minutes, lethargically moving around the court and halfheartedly putting up what seemed like purposeless shots, I gathered them together for our pre-practice talk. That is when I told them about the phone call I had just received from the NABC and of Aaron's award. The entire mood of the gym immediately changed.

Aaron, always humble, was his normal pleasant self, but it was the reaction of the other players that was so amazing. They were very proud and genuinely excited for him. There was no apparent jealousy, or faked enthusiasm, as there sometimes is when one player on a team is singled out for an award. In this case, their reaction, much like my own, was sincere.

That day, we went on to have one of the best practices I can remember. It was a practice that included more high fives and general expressions of affection towards fellow teammates than I had ever seen before. The players were happy for Aaron, and their emotions showed it.

Flashback to that turbulent flight home from Dallas knocking me around the cabin, thinking about the moment I first told the team of Aaron's award. It occurred to me that Aaron Patrick was a beloved teammate. He was beloved because he was a *good* teammate. I decided at that very moment that this was the advice I wanted to pass onto to my daughters. *Be a good teammate.*

It is all encompassing. Good teammates serve a higher calling. Good teammates put the team ahead of themselves, and that inevitably leads to making sound, unselfish decisions. As I would soon learn, people who serve the needs of others find purpose in their life, and that leads to perpetual happiness and self-satisfaction. Beyond that, good teammates are always in demand. Companies are always looking to hire good teammates—employees who prioritize the needs of the company over their own. The demand certainly isn't limited to just companies.

A neighborhood is a team. A school is a team, and so is family. The list goes on and on. Everybody is part of a team in some capacity, and the world cannot have too many good teammates.

The most difficult part of my job as a coach is not recruiting, strategizing game plans, dealing with over-involved parents, or anything along those lines. It is the day I have to notify the players who participated in the team's open tryout that I have to cut them. Nobody wants to be told they are not good enough for something, which in essence is what I am doing when I cut a player. I always feel like I am crushing their dreams. I accept that it is a necessary part of the coaching profession, but nonetheless, it is a part I do not enjoy.

I try to handle the process in as dignified a manner as possible. I don't callously post a list of the players who made the team on a wall or website, and I don't celebrate the players who made the team in front of those who did not. At the conclusion of the tryout, I gather everyone together and then ask for a select few to stay behind before dismissing everyone else. The ones remaining behind are almost always the players being cut. I meet with each of those players individually. I try to explain to the player why I did not select him, offer suggestions of what he could work on to improve his chances of making the team next time, and then offer to answer any questions he may have.

When Aaron Patrick tried out for the team his freshman year, he was one of the players I asked to stay behind. Aaron was not an especially skilled player at that point. He was a five-foot-nothing guard from the town of Johnsonburg, Pennsylvania, which is a little over 80 miles southeast of Erie. The town, which is known for the distinct smell of its paper mill, has a total population of around 2,400.[2] It is far from being a sports Mecca.

I had already made up my mind that I was going to keep Aaron on the team that year. I knew he wasn't probably talented enough to be a contributor yet, but I saw potential. There was just something Rudy Ruettiger-esque about him that I admired. He was humble, hardworking, driven, and seemed to get along with everyone.

I asked him to stay behind because I wanted him to know that he espoused the qualities of players I respected. I also wanted to caution him to never abandon those qualities, even when he got discouraged, which I expected he might because I anticipated limited playing time in his near future. I can now write with complete honesty that not once over the next four years of his college basketball career did his efforts and attitude ever wane.

Aaron was the last of the players I asked to stay behind to meet with me. When he walked into the room, he was noticeably nervous and reluctant to make eye-contact. He seemed dazed and stared at the floor. He was expecting the worst.

I initiated the conversation by saying, "Aaron, normally, I bring kids in here to tell them why they didn't make the team. However, I wanted to bring you in here to tell you exactly why I am putting you on the team." He looked up at me, having comprehended that I would not cut him, and then started to cry. I think his tears were part relief and part exhilaration that he was going to be a member of the team. He shook my hand, thanked me, and walked out of the room. That is how it all began.

The people handling the Good Works Team Award from the NABC, and even more so, Allstate Insurance were fantastic. They treated the recipients superbly and had arranged a memorable, all-expenses-paid trip for them. They flew Aaron to Dallas, put him up in a luxury hotel, and fed him meals far better than what most college students are accustomed to eating. Along the way, Aaron got to rub shoulders with basketball and celebrity royalty.

The members of the Allstate Good Works Team officially received their awards during the NABC's Guardians of the Game award show. This is the black-tie equivalent to the sport of basketball's Oscars or Emmy awards. The culminating experience for the recipients, though, was when they were recognized on center court during the Kentucky versus Wisconsin national semi-final game at the Final Four.

Adding to the ambiance of the event was the fact that the game was played in front of the largest crowd ever to watch a live college basketball game and on the most impressive stage imaginable—the Dallas Cowboys Stadium. I had seen the stadium on television before and once watched a documentary on the building of the facility. But until you walk into that massive arena and see that humongous 60-yard video screen, you cannot fathom how big and glorious it is.

As the award recipients walked onto the floor, I got the sense that the players from more recognizable schools like Michigan, Ohio State, and Virginia were not as ecstatic to be there. I can only assume that it was more bittersweet for them, like a consolation prize, as they had all played on teams who made the tournament that year and were not that far removed from playing on the court where they now stood, as eliminated participants. That wasn't the case for Aaron Patrick.

My eyes started to well up and tears slowly seeped down my cheeks when they announced Aaron's name. He gave a confident wave to the crowd. I chuckled and thought back to that day of tryouts his freshman year when he cried after I informed him that he was not getting cut from the team. Things had truly come full circle. I once read that tears shed for yourself are a sign of weakness, but tears shed for another are a sign of strength. If that is true, then I was the strongest coach on the planet at that moment. I was so happy for him.

In a way, Aaron winning that award did more for me and my coaching philosophy than I could have ever imagined. For a long time, I was a *transactional* coach. I undervalued my platform and failed to use my position to benefit anyone other than myself. I had no interest in viewing players as anything but a commodity to be used for the sole purpose of advancing my career agenda and enhancing the pleasure I received from winning games or, worst of all, validating my existence. If I helped a player, it was because I thought it would come back to help me. I was, in the truest form, a *transactional* coach.

If you do this for me, I'll do that for you. Nothing more. Nothing less. Play well and help me achieve status, and I'll give you praise and attention. Play poorly and I'll scream and humiliate you, which will also give me status as a coach who is "tough" on his players. Naturally, I expected immediate gratification from the transaction because I lacked the patience and wisdom to appreciate what beauty can come through the player/coach relationship over time.

I first came across the term "transactional coach" while reading Joe Erhmann's book *InsideOut Coaching. Parade* magazine called Erhmann "the most important coach in America" in August 2004 for his commitment to using the sport of football as a vehicle to teach manhood.[3] His book was a spinoff of the Jeffrey Marx New York Times Bestseller *Season of Life*, written several years earlier.

A Pulitzer-prize-winning journalist, Marx reunited with Erhmann, his childhood hero and former star of the NFL's Baltimore Colts, to tell the inspirational story of the Gilman High School football team's journey into manhood. Marx was a waterboy for the Colts and adored Erhmann as a youngster. However, a lot had changed since Marx last saw his hero. Erhmann had become an ordained minister and was no longer the life-of-the-party, wild man that Marx once knew. He now served a higher cause as a volunteer high school football coach, and was using sports to teach life and challenge society's traditional benchmarks of masculinity.[4]

In *InsideOut Coaching*, Erhmann goes into more detail on the subject of how young men are taught falsely about masculinity and how coaches fail to use their position to transform the lives of their players. Many of the issues addressed in Erhmann's book applied to me. Reading it made me want to be a better coach, a different kind of coach. I like to think I had already started down that path by the time Aaron came to play for me.

Aaron winning the award set into motion a sequence of events that allowed me to stop tiptoeing down that path and forge full speed ahead with the momentum of a freight train. On that bumpy flight when I decided what advice I wanted to pass onto my daughters should that turbulence bring my life to a sudden end, I had no idea what the future had in store for me.

The phrase "be a good teammate" consumed my every thought. It crept into almost every conversation I had. I became as obsessed with relaying that advice to everyone I came in contact with as I had formerly been with making it into the March Madness tournament. I felt so strongly about those words and the effect they could have on someone's life, and on society in general, that I was compelled to spread the message.

If I was invited to speak at a banquet, I brought the "be a good teammate" message with me. If I conducted a clinic at a school, or if I was at a summer camp, I made sure I talked about being a good teammate to the kids. I explained why they should be good teammates and how they could benefit from being good teammates. I explained how good teammates are always in demand. At one point, though, one elementary school student asked me a very honest question: What *is* a good teammate?

It occurred to me that I needed to precisely define what a good teammate was, and this proved to be a harder task than I had anticipated. I wanted a definition simple enough for an elementary student to understand and remember, yet inclusive enough to have meaning to a player or coach in the prime of his career. I wanted it to be something in the realm of Robert Fulghum's book from the 1980s, *All I Really Need to Know I Learned in Kindergarten.*

One of the reasons it was hard for me to come up with a definition was because I don't think I was ever really a good teammate when I was a player. I thought I was, but in context with the definition that I eventually decided upon, I am certain I wasn't.

Good teammates care above all about the team, and they care about the feelings of their teammates. I was not raised, nor encouraged, to be a good teammate when I was younger, at least not in the sense of putting the needs of the team ahead of my own. I was brought up to be too competitive with my teammates and too individualistic to put the team ahead of my personal goals.

Some of my worst memories growing up are of the car rides home after my games. They were painful for me. My father insisted on offering his opinions about how I played as soon as we got in the car. He was relentless in critiquing my performance. The outcome of the game and how the team performed were of such little importance to him that he hardly ever mentioned them. It was all about how many points I scored, how many tackles I had, or how many home runs I hit.

I came to hate the car rides because there was no escaping his criticism. Trapped in the car, I had to sit and take it. Sometimes, he would take notes during the game and hand me the notes when we got in the car. He would then explain his notes in agonizing detail.

As bad as he acted afterward, he was often worse during the games. He would bark instructions from the bleachers, yell at the referees, and openly berate the coaches. In hindsight, it is surprising how readily he would undermine the authority of the coach, considering he had himself been a coach.

I vividly recall an occasion during my older brother's senior season of high school football when my father got so upset at the coach that he left the stands and came down to the sideline. He yelled at the coach and demanded they give the ball to my brother more often. It was embarrassing, especially for my brother. The coach that he called out happened to be everyone's favorite teacher and a wonderful mentor to many students at our school. He was undeserving of the things my father yelled at him. My brother was practically in tears during the incident.

Unfortunately, it was not the only time this type of episode happened with my father. There were many of them over the years, and as I came to realize, they were never actually about me or my brothers. They were about him.

He did not act like that because he was concerned about our feelings or the quality of our sports experience. He did it because of how it made him feel. My father did not like how he felt when we did not score the most points, when we were not the stars of the game.

Considering how miserable those post-game car rides were for me, it is not shocking that I put so much effort into trying to please him. I competed hard with my teammates so that I could be the leading scorer and gain my father's approval. This caused me to turn into the type of player who would be visibly depressed after a game because I had a bad shooting night, even though our team pulled off a huge upset win. I didn't care about how my teammates felt.

Aaron Patrick was not like that. He cared. He cared deeply about his teammates and the team. He didn't always get to play a lot of minutes in our games, but he was always into them, waving a towel and cheering from the bench.

There would be games where we suffered a tough loss, and although he never got a second of court time, he would be somber afterward in the locker room. Most kids who do not get into the game don't act that way. They usually have the attitude of, "I didn't get to play, so I really didn't have anything to do with us losing." There is an emotional detachment. If they are somber, it is usually feigned so they don't irritate one of the players who did get into the game. Aaron Patrick's solemnness was genuine.

One time another player on our team reached a career scoring milestone. Aaron was so thrilled with his teammate's accomplishment, that you would have thought Aaron was the player who broke the record. He cared about his teammates that much.

The notion that *good teammates care* eventually became the foundation of a three-sentence explanation of what I believe defines a good teammate: *Good teammates care. Good teammates share. Good teammates listen.*

The origins of the other two sentences (*Good teammates share. Good teammates listen.*) were the product of my research, experiences, and willingness to absorb the wisdom of those who possessed a better understanding of life than I did. Trust is what links all three sentences. The *teammate/teammate* and *coach/teammate* relationships are built on trust. For there to be a good teammate, there must be trust.

As I dived into the challenge of defining a good teammate, I was forced to examine the virtue of trust. Everybody has an opinion on what trust is and what defines it. Words like "respect," "believe," and "confidence" are typically used to describe the meaning of trust. For players, the meaning of trust is often a misplaced belief in the amount of freedom their coach gives them on the court or field. For example, "My coach does not trust me to shoot the ball from the three-point line," or "My coach does not trust me to guard that player."

But those are only examples of performance-based trust. They have little to do with relationship-based trust—*real* trust. Players sometimes have a hard time differentiating between the two. The misunderstood difference is in the motive. Understanding intent is at the heart of trust and a productive, healthy relationship. Those who desire trust must make an effort to understand the intent of the action, and not just the result of the action. This can be difficult for coaches since the nature of the profession is so results oriented.

Players hardly ever set out with the intention of deliberately doing something wrong, but coaches typically react as though they did. When coaches ask *why*, they make an effort to discover intent and can then understand the action. Understanding leads to empathy, which leads to trust. Good teachers, good coaches, and good teammates all grasp this concept.

In the history of sports, there may not exist a more difficult time than the present for coaches to get their players to trust them. In the wake of the Jerry Sandusky abuse scandal at Penn State University, and the almost endless supply of media reports of athletic scandals, today's player is predisposed to be skeptical of a coach's motives, and perhaps rightfully so. Recent data certainly supports this.

The results of a survey released at the 2014 NCAA Convention shed light on a growing and otherwise unsettling problem for coaches, particularly men's basketball coaches. According to the Study of Student-Athlete Social Environments, basketball coaches are less trusted by their male players than any other collegiate sport. Of the more than 20,000 student athletes surveyed, men's basketball players had the lowest levels of trust in their coaches. Only 53% of the men's basketball players polled agreed with the statement: "My coaches can be trusted."[5]

Those numbers are clearly reflective of more than just a statement on performance-based trust. When nearly half of the players surveyed state that they don't trust their coaches, it is indicative of a much bigger problem.

As a society, we need mentors. That is what helps our young people grow. That is how knowledge is passed down and how the molding of philosophies occurs. Coaches are mentors, and if the mentee cannot trust the mentor, how will growth ever happen? Without trust, the mentorship process breaks down. Without trust, the team breaks down.

Perhaps a lack of trust is a trait of the millennial generation. Shortly after the results of the NCAA study were released, a survey conducted by the Pew Research Center showed that millennials have incredibly lower levels of trust than previous groups. In response to the survey question: "Generally speaking, would you say that most people can be trusted or that you can't be too careful in dealing with people," only 19% of millennials believed that most people can be trusted, compared to 40% of baby boomers.[6]

I can only theorize that this lack of trust is likely the result of a combination of a number of different generational social variances. These include elevated divorce rates, around-the-clock news coverage, the explosion of social media outlets, the vast amount of information now available on the Internet, and the necessity to fact-check the vast amount of information on the Internet. All of this, and much more, has contributed to a general lack of trust.

Take, for instance, the influence of the Internet. Suppose that in the middle of a conversation, a person makes some type of bold declaration, like their neighbor struck out Babe Ruth in 1923. That's an interesting bit of trivia, but is it true? In previous times, people would base their trust in that statement largely on the prior interactions they have had with the speaker. If the person has established himself as a straight shooter, then people would probably believe him. If he had a reputation for telling tall tales, then they will be far less likely to do so.

Today, the moment the words come out of the speaker's mouth, everyone listening pulls out their smartphones and searches the Internet for verification. The reputation of the speaker is far less factored into the believability of the statement. Ironically, and probably inevitably, the moment the statement was proven to be true, someone in the group would still be skeptical. If there is still one true fact, it is that you cannot believe everything you read on the Internet. This is the conundrum faced by the millennials. They have never known anything but this way of thinking. Unfortunately, as the actions of this generation affect all of us, everyone is steadily gravitating toward this same mindset.

In order to imprint the concept of being a good teammate, the issue of trust must be addressed. The source of the mistrust (the Internet, social media, divorce rates, etc.) is not likely to be resolved. That horse is already out of the stable. Effort must be put into finding ways to teach trust.

As I searched for a definition of a good teammate, I was forced to explore the presence of trust in my coaching methods and in my relationships with my players. I thought about how Aaron demonstrated trust, and I began to search for answers about how I learned this virtue.

I searched specifically for the answers to three questions: How do you trust? How do you build trust? How do you earn trust? Each of those topics seemed to align with my definition of a good teammate (*Good teammates care. Good teammates share. Good teammates listen*). To be a good teammate may not have been how I was raised, but I learned how to become one. Interestingly, my journey of discovery revealed that the people who taught me to be a good teammate were some of the same people who taught me how to have, build, and earn trust. I didn't know I was learning it at the time, but I clearly was.

This brought me to the conclusion that a disconnect exists between the potential positive life skills learned through participation in sports and in how players are coached. Few players ever go on to make a living playing sports. Of the half-million boys currently participating in high school basketball, less than 1% of them will go on to participate at the Division I level. Of the approximately 4,000 draft-eligible college basketball players, an average of only 47 will be drafted by an NBA team. That equates to a .009% chance of a high school athlete being drafted to play professionally.[7] There are lotteries that have better odds.

Yet, there is nothing particularly shocking or revolutionary about those numbers. They are widely accepted as fact. Opponents of organized sports have leaned on those statistics for years as a means to diminish the role sports should play in society and to underscore the absurdity of the amount of time invested in amateur sports.

Athletic proponents always counter the longshot statistical argument by pointing out the invaluable intangibles learned through participation in sports—self-discipline, work ethic, resiliency, and, of course, teamwork. As coaches, do we really make a deliberate effort to specifically teach those intangibles? The likelihood of a player absorbing some of those intangibles certainly exists. However, explicitly targeting their integration into the athlete's participatory experience through our coaching methods rarely happens.

For most coaches, the often-cited "intangibles" are a defensive tool, wielded only when the need arises to justify our methods. Far more often than not, we coach teams with the intention of elevating the elite—those who might have a chance to make a career playing sports.

We model our coaching methods and strategies after professional sports and major college sports. Let's face it, with so much money now involved in BCS-level Division I sports, they might as well be considered professional sports. Winning is the primary objective at that level.

Coaching like this is the equivalent of teaching an entire classroom with the intention of getting only the best and brightest students into graduate school at an Ivy League university and an eventual job at Google or Apple. In doing so, the teacher would abandon the education of the remaining majority of the class who do not possess the intellectual capacity to make it to that level. However, that is exactly how we coach amateur sports.

Perhaps in an attempt to address the disconnect, a movement has gained momentum that tries to negate at least one of the less appealing aspects of sports participation—exclusion. The so-called "everybody gets a trophy" leagues are growing in prominence. The philosophy is to plant the seed in the participant that everyone is special and everyone is a winner. These leagues aim to boost the self-esteem of the players by making them feel good about themselves. Players get trophies just for participating. But there is a problem with this philosophy too—it is not practical. The real world is not like that.

Sports participation governed by these means leads to disillusionment and to players learning inapplicable life skills. Not everybody wins in the real world. Disappointment and failure are entities that players will most certainly have to deal with in their lifetimes. Sports participation can teach players to handle failure and the important skill of resilience. Regardless of their intentions, the "everyone gets a trophy" leagues are thwarting some of the most important lessons learned through sports participation.

Coinciding with this contention is the belief that we are building a nation of entitled "wimps" through these leagues, where kids will later lack the toughness needed to handle life's challenges. Recently, James Harrison, an outspoken linebacker for the Pittsburgh Steelers and former NFL Defensive Player of the Year, took to social media to tell the story of how he made his young sons, ages 6 and 8, return the "participation" trophies they received.

Harrison wrote the following on his Instagram account. "While I am very proud of my boys for everything they do and will encourage them till the day I die, these trophies will be given back until they EARN a real trophy...I'm not about to raise two boys to be men by making them believe that they are entitled to something just because they tried their best...cause sometimes your best is not enough, and that should drive you to want to do better."[8]

I applaud Harrison's willingness to take a stance, and I agree with his thoughts on the "everybody gets a trophy" approach. But there is no definitive data supporting the alternative idea that emphasizing competiveness and superiority creates well-adjusted adults or guarantees a greater level of success in the real world, either.

However, the coaching method that would assure the highest probable degree of sustained success in life for the largest majority of players is accentuating the importance of being a good teammate. This should be our paramount charge in coaching amateur sports. I'd like to think that this is something that James Harrison could accept. Being competitive and earning something can be part of being a good teammate and are certainly not counter to it.

In my experience, and often echoed by those who have enjoyed documented success greater than I, winning is a byproduct of doing things the right way. It is not an actual destination. Compromising ethics or the learning opportunity of a teachable moment to earn the win is not necessarily a victory. Coming up short on the scoreboard because the coach taught a life lesson can be an enormous victory.

Aaron Patrick's accomplishment inspired me and sent me on an expedition to discover what it meant to be a good teammate. At times, the expedition was hard. I was forced to confront memories I had long ago suppressed and reopen old wounds that had never healed. It also made me receptive to a different way of thinking and to become a better coach...and a better person.

While defining what it means to be a good teammate is worthwhile, it is only part of the mission. Knowing *what* and *why* are meaningless without knowing *how*. I knew we needed more good teammates, and I came to define what a good teammate is, but I wanted an action plan to get people, mainly those from the millen-

19

nial generation, to become good teammates. As fate would have it, someone even further removed from the millennial generation than myself was the one who provided the most insightful direction in this endeavor.

Sister Eric Marie Setlock—*that* nun—is an incredibly blessed individual. She has been a member of the religious order of the Sisters of Mercy for over half of a century, yet her ability to connect with millennials seems to transcend the age gap. She possesses an uncanny ability to make people feel immediately at ease in her presence, which I learned is often the start of relationship-based trust.

As the Mount Aloysius College basketball team's most loyal fan, Sister Eric Marie cares intensely about our players and takes a sincere interest in their lives. She routinely asks me how a player is doing and is astute at noticing even the slightest change in a player's demeanor. Sister Eric Marie reads body language with the precision of an FBI profiler—a gift I have yet to receive as a coach.

I set out on a quest to find a way to encourage people to become better teammates, and I unintentionally stumbled across a virtual gold mine in the practices of this unassuming woman. What started out as simply observing her interact with the players after games and in the campus hallways evolved into me studying her with great diligence. This progressed to me deliberately seeking her counsel, probing for even more understanding.

Somewhere along the line, I dropped my guard enough for Sister Eric Marie to get into my heart. She allowed me to go back and reexamine the relationships I had with my coaches and mentors— the men of my personal Mount Rushmore—with greater clarity. More importantly, she showed me how I could get players to become good teammates and fueled me with the energy and passion needed to start a movement of change.

To get to that point, and to fully understand her, I had to start at the beginning of my coaching foundation. I needed to explore the origins of why I coached the way I did and the events that shaped the way I viewed the relationship between the words trust and teammate.

2

IRON MAN—THE FIRST FACE ON MY MOUNT RUSHMORE

I HAD an unusual upbringing, and that left me with the capacity to start several sentences like few others. Here are some examples.

When our lion bit his finger off…
One time, my neighbor the moonshiner…
Since our ship was anchored to the top of the mountain…
Because the bear made me late for practice…

This unique "ability" was the byproduct of the decisions made by my eccentric father. Like most men, my first coach, the person who initially taught me about manhood and life—and trust—was my father. But unlike most men, he really was a coach. He was also, at times, a monster.

My father, Jack Loya, is the first face on my personal Mount Rushmore. He was born December 26, 1940, in the shadows of the steel mills of Johnstown, Pennsylvania. Located about 60 miles east of Pittsburgh, Johnstown—in addition to its steel heritage—is usually known for two things: The Great Flood of 1889 and the Paul Newman hockey movie, *Slapshot*.

The devastating flood of 1889, one of America's first national disasters, killed over 2,000 people and was the first major relief effort for Clara Barton and the American Red Cross.[9] The movie *Slapshot* is a cult classic for sports fans. It is about a semi-pro hockey team and its ties to the closing steel mills in the fictitious city of Charlestown. It was filmed in Johnstown and was loosely based on the life of a former Johnstown Chiefs minor league hockey player.[10]

My father was the second and youngest child of John and Lucille Loya. My grandfather, John, was a well-liked and well-respected member of the community. Born to Slovakian immigrants, his family initially settled outside of Philadelphia. Their farm occupied the land where the world-famous King of Prussia Mall presently stands. As it is the nation's largest retail shopping complex, that property is worth considerably more these days.[11] Alas, my ancestors sold that land long before it ever materialized into anything relative to its current value.

Shortly after my grandfather was born, my great-grandfather took a job with the Cambria Steel Company and moved the family west to the then-thriving city of Johnstown. Thousands of Eastern European immigrants had settled in this area and gained employment in the mills and coal mines. My great-grandfather worked in Cambria's coal mining division.

It was an incredibly difficult job. In those pre-union days, he endured cruel working conditions and long work days. He reported for work before sunrise, spent the day in a pitch-black mine, and emerged long after sunset. Weeks at a time would pass without him ever seeing daylight. Unfortunately, this was a common occurrence for his trade, and it often contributed to a common problem—alcoholism.

Those who knew my grandfather often commented that he had a hard life growing up. This was typically attributed to my great-grandfather's drinking. Money was tight in their family, and regular meals were far from the norm. The difficult nature of the coal-mining profession made the drinking understandable, but it nevertheless exacerbated their family's situation.

Growing up in Johnstown, however, was a much different experience for my grandmother, Lucille. She lived on the outskirts of town, and her father worked for the railroad. They lived on a farm with chickens and a flourishing garden. Food was plentiful in their home.

The Depression was in full swing, so John and Lucille's lack of money was something they had in common. Although she had enough food to eat, Lucille only had one dress to her name. The embarrassment of not having sufficient school clothes, coupled with her mother's need for help raising the other siblings in her family, led to her dropping out of school in the eighth grade.

John graduated from Johnstown Catholic High School. He loved sports and excelled in his athletic endeavors. Like others before him, and many after, athletic prowess was a means for my grandfather to compensate for his family's financial and social shortcomings and to establish an identity for himself.

Of the many things that have changed over the years in sports, the belief that social status and identity can be gained through athletic achievement is definitely not one of them. That connection still exists and may realistically be one of the factors explaining why modern athletes are less trusting.

A Pew Research Center analysis conducted in 2007 identified low-income adults and minorities—two of the more prominent groups who historically participate in sports and would conceivably seek identity through athletic prowess—as having lower levels of trust than any other social cohort.[12] Reinforced by similar surveys, sociologists often find individuals who come from disadvantaged backgrounds feel it is too risky to trust others because they lack the means to handle the outcomes of misguided confidence. In layman's terms, they can't afford to trust.

In the Depression era of my grandfather's childhood, the alternative to gaining identity through sports was to risk having nothing at all. I suspect that was why he worked so hard to excel in athletics and excel he did. He played on countless sports teams and experienced considerable success. Once, during high school, John and another teammate won an entire track meet by themselves. John did all of the running events, and his teammate did all of the jumping and throwing events. It was a spectacular accomplishment.

Despite his athletic achievements, John was an otherwise reserved and very conservative man. He was also exceptionally hard working and intelligent, far beyond his level of education. Determined to earn employment before marrying Lucille, John studied rigorously for a civil service exam that was offered for a pair of openings at the Johnstown post office. Out of more than a thousand applicants, he scored the second highest on the exam. John retired as a postman nearly 40 years later. It was a testament to the value he placed on commitment and loyalty.

My father shared my grandfather's love of sports, and also excelled in sports as a youth. What he did not share, though, was my grandfather's cautious nature, a dissimilarity that would cause our family considerable stress over the years.

My father graduated from Clarion State College where he was a four-year letterman on the football team. He played both offensive and defensive end, as well as special teams. The rarity at which he came off the field earned him the nickname "Iron Man."

After graduation, he received more than a few letters from NFL teams inviting him to what would be today's equivalent of free agent camps. However, a nagging shoulder injury ultimately ended his brief stint with the Baltimore Colts organization.

My parents met while my father was taking graduate classes at West Virginia University. My mother was almost nine years his junior and still a high school student at the time. He had already begun his foray into the coaching world by the time they met. Considering his football background, it was ironic that basketball piqued his coaching interest. He started as an elementary coach, then moved up to the high school varsity level. He was coaching at Frederick Community College in Maryland when my brother was born and had moved on to Barrackville High School in Fairmont, West Virginia by the time I came around.

He would go on to coach several other high school and small college teams before eventually retiring as a high school physical education teacher. I loved going to my father's games as a kid. It made me see the game differently, including how much went on behind the scenes. His players were my heroes growing up. I idolized them more than they will ever know. Some of them went on to live very interesting lives. For instance, Stacy Porter, who was an undersized center for one of my father's junior college teams, went on to become a secret service agent and guarded President Bill Clinton during his time in office.

Unfortunately, it was my father's off-court antics that had an even bigger impact on my life. Against my grandfather's wishes, my father sought a career change and purchased The Ship Hotel in the mid-70s. It was a disastrous venture that forever altered the course of an otherwise foreseeable Rockwellian future for my family.

The S.S. Grand View Ship Hotel was an architectural wonder with a fascinating history. In 1913, American entrepreneur Carl Fisher, perhaps best known for paving his famous Indianapolis Motor Speedway with bricks and starting the Indy 500, saw an opportunity when he proposed the nation's first coast-to-coast roadway. Fisher spearheaded efforts to build what would come to be known as the Lincoln Highway, a continental roadway stretching from New York City to San Francisco.[13]

With the construction of the highway well underway, a Dutch immigrant by the name of Herbert Paulson saw an entrepreneurial opportunity of his own. Paulson had been advancing with the construction crew as they cleared the road's path, selling sandwiches to the hungry workers. When the construction reached a particular point in the Allegheny Mountains of western Pennsylvania, Paulson fell in love with the breathtaking view and set up a permanent roadside establishment selling refreshments to passing motorists.

The original building was built in the shape of a castle, a tribute to Paulson's European lineage. But Paulson's love of the sea, coupled with the way the early morning fog settled in the valley, leaving only the highest peaks exposed like tiny islands, led him to remodel the building to resemble a full-fledged ocean liner. Paulson took the nautical theme to the extreme, adding smoke stacks to the building's roof, having the employees dress in traditional maritime garb, and even referring to parts of the building by their more common nautical names.

In its heyday, The Ship Hotel welcomed the Who's Who of the world's rich and famous because for celebrities traveling east, it was typically the final stop before reaching New York City. Will Rogers, Thomas Edison, Greta Garbo, J.P. Morgan, Henry Ford, and President Calvin Coolidge were among the hotel's famous guests. When I was a kid, it used to be fun to look through The Ship Hotel's old guest books and try to find the signatures of famous people.

By the time my parents bought the building and its accompanying 100-plus acres, the business's decline in popularity was already well underway. The opening of the Pennsylvania Turnpike, just a few miles to the south, had taken considerable traffic away from the more mountainous Lincoln Highway and the iconic landmark known as The Ship Hotel.

Our family, which included my older brother and younger sister, took up residency in The Ship Hotel in 1978. We would welcome two more siblings into our clan while living there. By modern resort standards, there were not that many guest rooms at The Ship Hotel. As my family lived in what would be considered some of the hotel's top-level rooms, the kind that powerbrokers would have stayed in during their visits, I shake my head knowing how likely it was that my bedroom was undoubtedly once the stateroom of Thomas Edison or Henry Ford or some other great American figure.

My father tried to run the business as-is for several years before making drastic changes to the structure. Travelers were not the only thing on the decline. The metal exterior of the building was deteriorating and starting to rust. My father decided to nail wooden planks over the metal and renamed the business Noah's Ark.

In keeping with the new theme, he also opened a small zoo adjacent to the hotel. It was a disaster from the start. Having lived through it, I can say with absolute certainty that the movie *We Bought a Zoo* and the book that inspired it do not even come close to capturing the experience!

There was a myriad of problems associated with the Noah's Ark undertaking, and given my father's lack of zoological knowledge, it was hardly a surprise. He tried to run it himself, and with dwindling finances and a growing family, corners were frequently cut.

In the beginning, he tried to keep things simple with a small petting zoo. There were rabbits, ducks, and other "cute" animals. At some point, we got a white-tailed deer. It was just a small fawn, but my father was worried about hunters mistakenly shooting it during deer season, so he brought it inside the hotel to live with our family. I remember the deer being very docile and playing with it as if it were a normal family pet.

My father also added a very grumpy goat to the zoo. I cannot say that I would have entirely objected to a hunter mistakenly taking a shot at that animal, though. The goat's name was Velvet, and it was flat-out mean. My father used to make my brother and me feed the animals in the evening. If we got distracted and inadvertently turned our backs on Velvet, we were all but guaranteed to get an unpleasant jolt in the backside, compliments of the goat's knobby horns.

Eventually, the zoo grew, and we acquired larger and more interesting animals. We had a bear that loved sweets, so my father would make a weekly trip to the local Hostess bakery and buy a load of their outdated products. That bear loved those sugary treats to the point that my father started reselling the outdated products to zoo visitors. For a few dollars, guests could launch Twinkies, Ho Hos, and Zingers down a pipe and into the bear's cage. Of course, it was not long until the bear developed a severe toothache. It died when a veterinarian my father brought in to treat the bear's ailment tranquilized it.

There were always characters hanging around the hotel, and my father would occasionally employ them for odd jobs. During the 80s, the Reagan administration began making cutbacks, which led to the nearby Somerset State Hospital releasing patients of questionable mental health. With no specific place to go, those patients started walking Route 30, the nearest road to the hospital, and eventually stumbled upon our hotel.

I cannot remember all of the characters, but I do recall a former mental patient named George, who had a weird obsession with scraping paint. He had a little knife and could not stand painted wood. My father gave him meals and let him sleep in the restaurant's vestibule at night in exchange for labor scraping the chipping paint off the building's deteriorating door frames.

The rural location of the business also contributed to more than a few peculiar personalities wandering in from Appalachia. My father allowed a recluse mountain man named Dean to live on the otherwise uninhabited property surrounding the hotel. Dean was a functional alcoholic and ran a moonshine still in those woods. Occasionally, he would emerge to offer his services.

One day, my father had Dean clean out the bear cage. He was supposed to lock the bear on one side of the cage while he cleaned the other. Somewhere in the process, and presumably due to Dean feeling the effects of over-imbibing his product, he fell asleep in the bear cage. It was an unusually busy day for the hotel, and sure enough, someone who came for lunch snapped a photo of Dean and the bear. The photo—and the accompanying embarrassment—made it into the pages of the local newspaper, thus giving the bear who liked sweets an added bit of notoriety.

Another time, Dean had been feeding our lion, and he came back into the restaurant sheepishly holding his hand. He had tried to pet the lion, who promptly bit off his finger. My father rushed him to the hospital. It took some time, but Dean eventually came to show off the remaining nub on his hand like a badge of honor. How many people can honestly say they had their finger bit off by a lion?

As for me, I hated that lion. It scared the daylights out of me as a kid. I suspect the average person cannot really comprehend what it feels like to be woken up in the morning by the roar of a hungry lion. I would lie motionless in bed, hiding under the covers, trying to figure out in the fogginess of just waking up if it was a nightmare or if this time the lion finally got free and was on the hunt. Either way, it was a horrifying experience.

Dean's finger incident with our lion is possibly not even our most compelling zoo story. We got most of the zoo's inhabitants from a man named Leonard Kiser who ran a wildlife ranch and was ready to part with some of his animals. Now and then,

I would go with my father to see Kiser's animals. On one of the more humorous excursions, Kiser tried to get my father to take a mischievous monkey who was removed from his previous zoo for excessive masturbation in front of the guests. No sooner did he explain to my father what the problem was with the monkey than the monkey gave a "demonstration" right there in front of us. Amazingly, we did not buy the monkey that day.

On another strange occurrence, a guy stopped to eat at the hotel and asked my father to consider taking his pet lion off his hands. He had a full-grown lion in the front seat of his car and was looking to part ways with it. I have no idea how he came to find my father or what brought him to our parking lot that day, but as unfathomable as it sounds, my father took the lion from him and put it in our zoo. Government regulations were much more relaxed back then.

As it turned out, the new lion was unusually temperamental and did not get along well with our other lion. My father eventually gave that lion away to another unfortunate soul, who took it home under the assumption that he was getting a domesticated animal. A short time later, the lion escaped from the new owner's house and roamed the streets of the town. The police had to put the lion down when it refused to release a neighborhood pet that it had captured.

As can be imagined, my more cautious grandfather did not approve of the environment in which we were being raised or of my father having these types of characters around his grandchildren. He could not find any value to it that outweighed the risk to our safety. Sadly, yet perhaps fortunately, my grandfather did not live long enough to see The Ship Hotel debacle reach its climax, nor the dreadful after-effects it had on our family.

The Lincoln Highway Heritage Corridor called The Ship Hotel "Lincoln Highway's most famous landmark."[14] It was even listed on the National Register of Historical Places.[15] One of the hotel's main attractions was its remarkable view. As very prominently advertised on the building's exterior, three states and seven counties could be seen from the hotel. I would often walk onto the deck and try to spot each of the states (Pennsylvania, Maryland, and West Virginia). The view was breathtaking.

Unfortunately, in October 2001, barely a month after one of the most horrific events in American history, and less than 10 miles from the Shanksville crash site where a group of brave passengers fought the terrorists who hijacked United Flight 93, The Ship Hotel burned to the ground. Officials ruled the incident as arson but were never able to make any arrests directly tied to the fire.

My father worked hard trying to restore the hotel. I cannot find fault in his work ethic. But as with most of his endeavors, he did things, for a lack of a better term, *half-assed*. The stress of running a failing business and the overwhelming workload took its toll on him. He became increasingly short-tempered and at times verbally and physically abusive. I long ago repressed many of those memories, apart from a few of which I cannot seem to rid myself.

One time, when I was probably five or six, my father was replastering a wall in the upstairs corridor. He had spent hours on the project. I was playing outside on the deck and came running inside to get something. Oblivious to what he had been working on, as children often are, I accidentally scraped his still wet plaster and messed up the pattern as I passed by the wall. When he saw what I had done, he kicked me in the back so hard I could not stand up straight. The pain was excruciating and left a huge bruise on my back. I remember trying to cry, but all I could muster was one of those near-silent cries where tears and facial expressions come, but no noise.

The worst part of the incident was that my mother saw the huge bruise on my back and knew what he did, but she did nothing about it. She let me believe that somehow I deserved what happened to me.

Another time, all of my brothers and sisters were packed into the back seat of my family's Honda station wagon. It was very cramped, and the car was far too small to carry a family of our size. My sister was sitting too close, or touching me funny, or doing some other action that I found annoying—hardly a shock for young siblings to fight over these types of things. My father had

had enough, though, and reached into the back seat and grabbed me by my head. He proceeded to bang my head back and forth between the back of his driver's side headrest and the front of my seat. It went on for what seemed like an eternity. When he was done, I was extremely dizzy.

As usually was the case when my father went off, my other siblings scrambled for safety. I recall looking at my older brother. His face did not show any expression of empathy or even fear. He just looked at me, as if to say, "You should not have done that because you should have known what he was going to do to you." It was such an accepting look he gave me, and it was dysfunction in its purest form.

I wonder now at what point I—and recalling the look on my older brother's face, he too—became so accepting of my father's rage. I think back to an experience I had with my daughter when we were potty-training her. She was probably barely two years old at the time and had come with me to my office. I was rushing to get things done and otherwise consumed in my stress when she declared she had to go to the bathroom. It was not the most convenient moment for her to have to go, but I still whisked her off the restroom.

She was less than cooperative and attentive while on the toilet, and I was not as patient as I should have been. Like a typical toddler, she was doing everything except sitting still and heeding my instructions. In my haste, I grabbed her by the arm to get her attention. In doing so, I must have unintentionally pinched the inside of her arm. She started to cry, but it wasn't her tears that got my attention.

Right before she cried, she let out a quick gasp, and then gave me the most surprised look. If that wasn't enough, in her sweet little innocent voice she stated with complete astonishment, "You hurt me." The look on her face when she said that will forever be etched in my memory. It was the first time in her life that she did not have complete trust in me. It was lost innocence.

Up to that moment, she had no idea that her daddy could or would hurt her. I realized that she would never trust me with the same level of wholeness. It saddened me, especially considering such a small unintentional act had caused her to lose trust in me.

I wondered what single event happened in my early childhood to cause me to first lose trust in my father.

Several years before flames consumed The Ship Hotel, our family had moved into a mobile home that my parents had put on the vacant acreage that originally accompanied their purchase of the building. For far too long, my parents and my four siblings had occupied a cramped three-room apartment on the hotel's top floor. Our new home was, by comparison, considerably roomier. Deep down, I think my parents knew they had to get our family out of the hotel. However, in their perceived necessity to escape, they moved us into even more difficult living conditions.

The mobile home was situated in the middle of the woods, which meant that visits from wild animals, including bears, were common. The first time you see a bear out your window, it is a little unnerving, but still interesting and even exciting. But given the prior experience we had with our zoo, the novelty of seeing a live bear on our doorstep wore off quickly. In fact, it became a nuisance. On more than one occasion, I was late to basketball practice because a bear would not allow us to get outside to our car.

There was not a neighbor within almost a one-mile radius of our new place, and the driveway leading to it epitomized the word "treacherous." It was a narrow dirt and shale road that spanned a steep ravine. Drivers literally risked their lives traversing it. The deep mud caused by rain made our driveway nearly impassable at times, as did the snow during the winter months. For those reasons, we usually parked our vehicles at the end of the long driveway and were forced to hike back and forth to our home.

As bad as the driveway was, it was not the worst part of our new living arrangements. My father did not drill a well. Instead, he tried to run a pipe to our home from a nearby natural spring located on the mountainside. Our family rarely had running water because of this arrangement. The pipe would freeze in the winter, and the natural spring would dry up in the summer. We had to survive the bulk of the time by filling dozens of plastic, gallon jugs with water we got from other locations. No hot showers. No flushing toilets. No washing clothes. It was a pioneering, primitive life-style, only this was not the 1890s—it was the 1990s.

"Pioneering" is too complimentary of a word to describe it. It was ridiculous. Walking that long muddy driveway left me to go to school every day covered in mud. Not being able to shower or con-sistently have clean clothes made me the stinky kid at school. In hindsight, I think one of the reasons I loved gym class and playing sports so much was because I got to take a shower at the school.

As the dysfunction in our household grew, so did our finan-cial woes. I give my parents credit, though, for at least taking gov-ernment assistance to keep our family fed. However, it was some-times an embarrassing experience. I hated how people looked at us whenever we paid for our groceries with food stamps. I hated how other kids stared at me whenever I had to stand in line at school to get my free lunch vouchers. And I hated the taste of the govern-ment welfare cheese my parents fed us.

I hated it so much because it did not have to be that way. It was frustrating to know that we brought that on ourselves. My parents both had college degrees and grew up in loving, normal homes. Sometimes people who grew up in poverty, but later advanced to a higher level of social and financial stability, comment that they never knew they were poor growing up. I did not feel that way. Our family was poor and dysfunctional, and I knew it.

At any rate, it all had a horribly adverse effect on my confi-dence and social skills. As typically is the case, I started acting out in school. It was never anything major, but all the same, school became a problematic experience for me. I had trouble with con-formity, and I had trouble with authority. Although the root of my mistrust in authority figures is clear to me now, I am sure that there were times when I was a difficult pupil. Like my grandfather before me, sports became my escape.

I am well aware of how bizarre all of this sounds. The stories of lions, a ship marooned on the top of a mountain, and a near twenty-first century home without running water are so outlandish that they push the limits of believability. They are nevertheless true, which begs one obvious question: What does any of it have to do with coaching?

Simple. It is the foundation I was given. Specifically, it is the baggage I brought with me as I entered the coaching profession. All of those experiences affected how I viewed and treated players. There is genuine truth in the theory that we are the product of our experiences.

I seriously doubt if any of my teachers, coaches, or even classmates knew the extent of what I endured every day just to get to school. Battling the mud and snow of that driveway was tough, and my father valued toughness. He thought any physical challenge was good for me because it made me tough, regardless of how ludicrous the circumstances surrounding the challenge.

For instance, there seemed to be a never-ending need to dig ditches to reroute the water runoff and keep our driveway from totally washing away. It felt like I always had a shovel in my hand. In some twisted attempt to make me feel proud of how sore my hands were from using a shovel, my father would look at my hands and tell me rough hands are what saved Jews in concentration camps. He would say the Germans would go down the line and determine which Jews to spare from the gas chamber based on how rough their hands were. This somehow proved they were capable of doing hard labor and had some greater value.

Once, when I was about nine years old, I got sick in the middle of the night and threw up all over myself and my bed. My mother was visiting relatives out of town with my other brothers and sisters, but I still instinctively called for help. My father finally woke up, took one look at me, and said something along the lines of it being disgusting, and I needed to get it cleaned up. He then went back to bed.

Making a nine-year-old kid clean up his own vomit is not building toughness. Having rough hands and living through all of my family's dysfunction did not make me tough. It made me calloused. There is a difference. Being calloused only gives you the propensity to endure hardships. Being tough empowers you to attack challenges and not fear limits. Toughness is the ability to demonstrate courage in spite of your weaknesses.

Whenever I started coaching, I placed the same high value on what I was raised to believe toughness was. However, I had the same problem as my father in that I could not differentiate between physical toughness and mental toughness. They were synonymous to me.

The great UCLA basketball coach, John Wooden, had a favorite quote: "Physical strength is measured by what one can carry; spiritual strength by what one can bear."[16] There is enormous accuracy in that. Often, understanding the difference between physical toughness and mental toughness is what allows a coach to make a connection with a player. In the coaching world, the ability to relate to players can be of value, but the ability to empathize is irreplaceable.

In terms of producing good teammates, coaches have to find ways to accentuate the importance of mental toughness, especially in regards to how it measures up to physical toughness. We typically tend to praise and recognize physical toughness at a much higher level, which can overshadow the significance of mental toughness.

A good example of this is when a coach praises the player who beat the opponent's defenders and scored the most points in the game without also praising the player who is happy for his teammate's achievement and responds appropriately. Isn't the player who suppresses the natural tendency to be jealous of his teammate conveying toughness too? His toughness is entirely mental, but it should be recognized for its benefit to the team. He is being a good teammate.

In the grand scheme of things, only one of those actions is valuable to the player when he or she is done with sports and gets on with his or her life's work. The ability to put a leather ball through a metal hoop is not an important skill in the corporate world, but being supportive of a coworker's accomplishment without jealousy or resentment is.

Coaches can train players to develop this more valuable life skill by merely acknowledging its occurrence. All it would take is for the coach to turn his head and mention to the rest of the players on the team how much he admired how supportive they were of the leading scorer and point out that their attitudes and reaction are what make this team great.

A recent article in *Psychology Today* examined the results of a human resource firm's study on employee engagement and affirmed that what most employees desire more than anything is recognition for their contribution. Of the employees surveyed, 83% responded that "recognition for contributions was more fulfilling than any rewards or gifts."[17]

Players on a sports team are no different. As an old saying goes, *We are what we repeatedly do.* If a coach wants a player to be happy with the accomplishment of a teammate, and in doing so to be a good teammate, then the coach needs to find a way to have that action repeated. Openly recognizing it and praising it is one method to increase the repetition of that action. Ultimately, the team benefits from this praise too because it promotes "chemistry." Teams with good chemistry are usually comprised of good teammates and enjoy team success.

I do not want to discount completely what I learned from my father and how he influenced me as a coach. For example, he knew how to manipulate resources and circumvent the system to get things done. He knew how to grease the tracks by making deals and bartering for things he could not afford.

When we lived in The Ship Hotel, he had no means to plow the snow from the parking lot. A normal business owner would have bought a machine to do the plowing or at least hired someone to do it, but, as I have already established, "normal" was not a word usually used to describe my father. His solution was to send me out to stand along the side of the road and hold up two beer bottles from the restaurant's bar whenever the State road truck drove by. It always worked. The driver would take a few swipes at the parking lot with his snow plow, and then he would roll down his window. I'd climb up and hand him the bottles, and he'd drive off without ever saying a word.

Over the years, I have utilized comparable methods as a coach with the maintenance staff and campus security, among others, to cut through the red tape that frequently stands in the way of getting things done. It has proven to be an invaluable skill. Unfortunately, a lot of what I learned from my father was what *not* to do. That is why the introduction of the other men on my Mount Rushmore was critical to my evolution as a coach and to my understanding of what it meant to be a good teammate.

My father put me in a situation where it was often about survival and self-preservation. You had to be constantly protective of what you had, especially your pride. He forced us to have family secrets to keep us from being ashamed or embarrassed, like concealing the fact that we did not have running water in our house. I was incapable of being a good teammate to anyone because of the contribution of those things. I had a hard time forming relationships and letting people get close to me. I couldn't trust others not to judge me or make me feel more ashamed.

Growing up in a big family further hindered my ability to be a good teammate. You wouldn't think that to be the case, but it was. When you come from a big family, you learn to compete at an early age. Everything in your life that matters revolves around competition—and it is not always healthy competition. You compete for bathroom time. You compete for privacy. You compete for food. If you are late getting up for breakfast, there might not be any left. If you are not standing in the kitchen the moment your mother brings the groceries into the house, the best snacks might be gone by the time you get there. Worst of all, you compete for your parents' affection.

Luckily, the next round of dominant male figures to enter my life didn't make me feel that way. That is how I started to learn, at least subconsciously, what it takes to be a good teammate.

3

COMING TO THE BRITISH— THE SECOND FACE ON MY MOUNT RUSHMORE

I DESCRIBED my childhood as "unusual," but "unconventional" may be a better choice. That is probably the most accurate and least offensive description of my childhood. On rare occasions, however, my father's eccentric ways did pay dividends. Such was certainly the case when I first came into contact with British basketball coach Mike Burton—face number two on my Mount Rushmore.

In Ken Blanchard's book *Trust Works!: Four Keys to Building Lasting Relationships*, he identifies the ABCD Trust Model as a means to create and rebuild trust between individuals. Blanchard, the distinguished co-author of the New York Times bestseller *The One Minute Manager* and one of the world's most influential leadership experts, explains the four keys as Able, Believable, Connected, and Dependable.[18]

He goes on to elaborate on each element, stating: "Able is about demonstrating competence. Believable means acting with integrity. Connected is about demonstrating care and concern for other people. Dependable is about reliably following through on what the leaders say that they are going to do."[19] While Mike Burton certainly embodied each of these elements of trust, he is the person who provided me with the best example of the first and most critical component of trust—the ability *to* trust.

After graduating from high school, I still had an unquenchable desire to play college basketball, and more specifically, to play in the NCAA Division I tournament. That was my dream. There was one problem, however—I was not a good enough player for that to happen.

I had no viable Division I offers, not even as an invited walk-on. My high school was far from being located in a basketball recruiting hotbed. It was a small, rural school that played in a league with a low standard of talent. It was not until years later when I got out of Bedford County and was exposed to more basketball that I realized just how low the standard was. At that time, there were no AAU or travel team options in my area to compensate for the lack of competition and exposure.

I did get some interest from some lower level Division II and III schools. Academically, I even received a scholarship offer to attend NYU's prestigious Tisch School of the Arts. None of them were feasible options, however, as they would not have allowed me to reach my ultimate goal of playing in the *Big Dance*. Sometimes I wonder how different, yet perhaps unfulfilling, my life would have turned out had I chosen the NYU film school route.

As graduation from high school neared, my father made calls on my behalf, seeking other options for me to make it as a Division I basketball player. He was a former college coach and had some experience in the process. Although I was always grateful for him making those phone calls, I was also surprised at how few people returned his calls or were willing to help. It boggled my mind that coaches would not take a chance on another coach's son. Maybe it was a general statement on the distrustful, cutthroat climate of college basketball, or maybe it was just a statement on how little other coaches trusted my father.

I continued to explore other options. Prep school might have been a legitimate direction to take, but we were poor and could never afford the high costs. Also, I definitely was not good enough for any decent prep school to waste a basketball scholarship on me. That left few traditional alternatives.

Then something unexpected materialized. Through a bizarre sequence of phone calls, we were put in contact with a coach from England named Mike Burton, who ran a professional basketball team called the Chester Jets. The team was based in Ellesmere Port, an industrial seaport just outside of the city of Liverpool, home of rock 'n roll legend *The Beatles*.

The Jets were a grassroots operation that had recently moved up to the country's top division—the BBL. It is technically the British Basketball League, but back then, it was known as the Budweiser Basketball League, after the league's primary corporate sponsor. As I became acquainted with the British culture, the sponsorship seemed fitting and even appropriate, because from what I observed, they drank a lot of beer.

My American instinct, however, found the sponsorship very odd. Players traveled to games with huge bags that had the Budweiser logo printed on them. During the games, they used Budweiser towels and water bottles. Every uniform had a Budweiser logo embroidered on it, and after the games, the visiting team always took several cases of Budweiser home with them on the bus. The casual intermingling of alcohol and athletics seemed almost countercultural to me. Imagine the Lakers or Celtics sporting a big Budweiser logo on the front of their uniforms. Wouldn't that be disconcerting?

I suppose my naiveté might have had something to do with my perception of it as odd. In time, I accepted it as the European way.

Mike Burton, whom I eventually came to know more fondly as Burt, offered to let me train with his team in exchange for working for the club. It was an unusual offer, especially considering that Burt's sole interaction with me up to that point had been limited to a few, very brief phone calls. No scouting services. No online video. Just the tone of my voice.

As I soon learned, however, the ability to trust his intuition was one of Burt's best skills. Taking a chance on me, and this unusual arrangement, was out of the ordinary for even my family—but not for Burt. The decision was calculated, weighed in his mind, and determined to be a worthwhile venture. He sought out win/win situations, and that was often how he got ahead. As my career as a coach has progressed, I have also tried to follow Burt's model of seeking win/win situations with players. Whenever conditions exist that allow for mutually beneficial circumstances, the necessity to insert motivation into the relationship is greatly reduced, and that in turn minimizes potential resentment and shapes trust.

Burt believed that people were inherently good and deserving of trust. From his perspective, people deserved at least an opportunity to demonstrate if they were trustworthy or not. This foreign, yet greatly welcomed, perspective was refreshing to me. It immediately put me on a pedestal and made me not want to let him down. It was different than the more traditional approach of having me, as a player, have to work hard to gain the coach's trust.

The September following my graduation from high school, I boarded a plane bound for England and a rendezvous with a remarkable man, who also happened to be a remarkable coach. Burt's coaching resume speaks for itself. He spent ten years as the head coach of the Jets and was named the BBL Coach of the Year after the 1996–97 season. That accomplishment alone is noteworthy because he was the only British coach in Great Britain's top league that year. All of the other coaches were Americans.

Burt would eventually step aside as the club's head coach and focus on his general manager duties while still serving as an assistant coach. Under his leadership, the club achieved tremendous success and won its first ever National Trophy in 2000. They would go on to win the National Trophy for the next four years in a row.

In Europe, championships are handled much differently than in America, and from my experience, it is a much better system. In America, we tend to have one final championship that every team is competing for and where there can only be one winner. In Europe, they have several championship competitions going on throughout the season. For instance, in the BBL, there are four pieces of hardware that the leagues' teams compete for each season—the BBL Trophy, the BBL Cup, the league Championship, and the Play-off championship. In 2002–03, the Jets completed what was famously known as the "Jet Wash" and won all four championships in the same year. It was an incredible accomplishment.

Outside of coaching and working with the Jets, Burt also coached several school teams. This arrangement is not uncommon in European basketball. His Ellesmere Port Catholic High teams were perennial powerhouses. In fact, Ellesmere Port Catholic High is the only school in Great Britain to win the equivalent of a national high school championship in all eight divisions of the school's competitions—boys U14, girls U14, boys U15, girls U15, boys U16, girls U16, boys U19, and girls U19. By European standards, specifically British Basketball standards, that is about as successful as it gets.

If we have learned anything from the recent Olympics, it is that there are some very talented and innovated basketball coaches on the international level. Burt belongs in this category. He could flat out coach. If he had been working his craft in America, he would have attained considerably more fame and have been a recognized name in the coaching profession.

I vividly remember walking out of the arrival's terminal at Manchester International Airport and seeing Burt holding up a cardboard sign with my name on it. He introduced himself. We shook hands. Then we started walking to his car—very swiftly. Burt hated waste.

He was especially averse to wasting time, and that made him incredibly efficient. He moved from one spot to the next with gusto. He also moved from one task to the next with the same expedience. Burt was able to get more done in less time than most men, and that gave him the opportunity to compete with others who had more resources at their disposal.

For example, the Jets could not match the same financial backing as some of the other BBL franchises. The Manchester Giants, the Jets' closest rival, were owned by American billionaire Bill Cook, who headed the Cook Group, a global medical device manufacturing firm. Cook was also on the board of trustees at Indiana University and a huge Hoosiers basketball supporter. This situation accounted for several of Bob Knight's former players gracing the Manchester Giants roster.

Burt did not have these advantages at his disposal, but he was able to do more with less and better than anyone. He did not have the luxury of calling up agents and negotiating contracts that he knew would be guaranteed by a billionaire owner. Burt had to find overlooked players or disadvantaged players (be it by size or experience) and then get them to compete against players who had every advantage—and get them to do it for far less pay.

That is where I came to be an asset for Burt. The Jets did not have enough money to afford an entire roster. Burt could always find five or six players to make his team competitive, but there were not always enough players for practice. I was a much-needed body for scrimmages and drills in practice.

I never played in any games with the Jets, as I was trying to preserve my amateur status based on my understanding of NCAA rules. My intention was to return eventually to play college basketball in America, so I used my time with the Jets as an opportunity to train with better talent and become a better player.

I participated in every practice and training session with the Jets. They were fantastic. Burt ran a good practice, and I got to compete at a relatively high level of competition. Being around the Jets was very beneficial to me. Burt had me live in the house with the other professional players on the team, several of whom were larger than life, some literally more so than others.

One player I became particularly close with was Alan Bannister, more commonly known as "Big Al." Alan stood 7' 5" and weighed well over 300 pounds. As big as he was, his personality was even bigger. He had a great sense of humor, and we got along marvelously. Alan had played collegiately at Oklahoma State on the same team as future New York Knicks star John Starks, and he had a brief stint with the Utah Jazz before joining the Jets. I loved listening to Alan tell stories about his time with the Jazz, particularly his off-court interactions with Hall of Famer Karl Malone.

Another player whose company I enjoyed was a point guard named Dana "Binky" Johnson. Binky frequently let me work out with him. It was clear he had been well-coached during his college career. He would have me do a drill and say his college coach used to make him do this or that. The more stories he told me about his college coach, the more fascinated I became. It got to the point where I was annoying Binky with all of my questions about how his college coach did certain things. As it turned out, Binky played at Canisius College for a then unknown coach by the name of John Beilein, who would go on to become the now famous coach at the University of Michigan.

My climb up the coaching ladder has not followed the typical model. For one thing, I have never been an assistant coach at any level, only a head coach. I was a varsity head coach at the high school level and then became a head coach at the collegiate level. But my opportunity to regularly probe Binky about John Beilein, coupled with all of the time I spent with Burt and the work he had me doing for the Jets, was tantamount to one of the finest basketball coaching apprenticeships imaginable.

During Jets games, Burt had me sit on the bench and help take stats, which caused me to think very analytically about the game. At that time, there were also not enough qualified people in that part of England to teach basketball, which was growing in popularity with the younger generations. Burt had me travel to schools around the area to teach basketball lessons. Sometimes I would teach during the middle of the day for a high school physical education class; other times, I would teach a group of kids at an afterschool program. Some of the schools he sent me to did not even have basketball hoops at their school. Burt would have me strap a portable metal hoop to the roof of our car and take it with me to do the training session.

As the coach, general manager, and part-owner of the team, Burt had to hustle to meet the financial obligations of the club. He was kind of like a modern day Celtic's great Red Auerbach in that regard. One of Burt's best sources of fundraising was to run what I came to call the McDonald's clinics. He would hold a coaching session in the afternoon for kids, then load them onto buses and transport them to a local McDonald's to eat. Afterward, he would bring them back to watch the Jets game, a classic Burt win/win scenario. Kids got coaching, which they wanted. McDonald's—a Jets corporate sponsor—got business, which they wanted. And, the Jets got rowdy young fans, which they needed. My job was to help coach at the clinic, and then supervise the kids while they were at McDonald's and the game.

Burt gained loyalty with those around him through the admiration of his work ethic. How hard he worked, and how much he got accomplished during the day, left a big impression on me, and almost everyone else. People could not look at Burt's efforts and not admire his energy. Whether or not they agreed with what he was doing, his work ethic was undeniable.

In hindsight, I now see that Burt was employing an invaluable coaching tool. He was not motivating, he was inspiring. Motivating players, either positively (*Win this drill, and we will take tomorrow off*) or negatively (*Lose this, and we will run sprints until we pass out*), is fleeting. It is like throwing a bucket of gasoline on a fire. There is an immediate boost to the flame, which can be of value, but eventually, the flame goes back to its original level. Inspiration, however, is like injecting the fire with an endless supply of propane. The flames grow bigger, and they stay that way much longer.

Burt credits his work ethic to his parents. His mother was a hard worker who always managed to keep herself busy. She encouraged him to embrace the same level of aversion toward inactivity. Burt's father was an interesting man. He was a common laborer in several industrial factories, but much of his outlook on life was shaped years earlier while he was a medic in the British Army during World War II.

His father was stationed in Singapore when the seemingly impenetrable British stronghold fell to Japan in February 1942, barely two months after the Japanese attack on Pearl Harbor. The elder Burton became one of the 30,000 British prisoners of war that the Japanese sent from Singapore to Thailand to build the infamous Thai-Burma Railway. Prisoners were crammed into metal railcars for the 5-day train ride north, before being forced to walk another 200 miles to their POW worksite.[20] More commonly known as the *Railway of Death*, the 1957 Oscar-winning-film *The*

Bridge on the River Kwai.[21] immortalized the story. In all, 13,000 allied POWs and another 100,000 native laborers died during the endeavor.[22]

As a POW for over three years, Burt's father endured extremely inhumane treatment. Prisoners were routinely beaten for even the slightest of infractions and given as little as eight ounces of rice for their daily rations. Having grown up under the tutelage of someone who was capable of surviving such appalling circumstances, it does not take long to see the origins of many of Burt's more admirable qualities, like his hatred of waste and the premium he placed on industriousness.

Burt valued hard work in much the same way as my father did. The difference was that Burt worked smarter, and with considerably more efficiency. Another one of Burt's methods for financing the Jets was to operate a residential basketball camp every summer. That camp is still the longest running basketball camp in England, and for many years, it was also the largest. I returned to England for numerous summers to work at it. Watching Burt run the camp was a genuine lesson in efficient management.

Other teams would hold their camps on university campuses and use the dormitory rooms to house campers. That can be an expensive undertaking. Burt rented out a local high school and housed the campers in classrooms. He would clear out the desks and chairs and fill the classrooms with cots used by the army during World War II, which he had bought for next to nothing from a surplus outlet. The campers loved the setup, as it added to the ambiance of the camp. Burt maximized his profits by thinking outside the box and not overcomplicating things.

His dislike for waste was, of course, very present at the camp. Burt would always tell the campers the same thing before dismissing them for meals: *Take as much as you want, but eat as much as you take.* This rule kept the waste of food to a minimum, thereby keeping down his expenses. He would also hire the school's cafeteria workers to come back over the summer to cook the food. However, he would not make them serve the same bland meals they routinely served throughout the year. He allowed them to cook and bake things they enjoyed making. The quality of the food became one of the best parts of camp. The workers were happy, and so were the campers. At the end of the week, Burt would present the cafeteria workers with flowers at the camp's award ceremony. No one ever recognized them like that. It was such a small and inexpensive gesture, but it paid big dividends.

One area Burt would never skimp on was in how he treated the camp's coaches. He did not pay the coaches anything above the going rate. In fact, it was probably at the lower end of the wage scale. But he found other ways to keep the coaches loyal. At the end of each camp day, Burt always had food and drinks ready. It was a way for him to express his daily appreciation for the coaches' efforts. He did not wait until the end of the week to do this, nor did he host one big coach's social in a more formal setting, as many camps tended to do.

The way Burt did it, coaches were rejuvenated nightly and came back the next morning ready to give an even more enthusiastic effort. The amount of time the coaches spent with each other when the camp day ended led to a more closely knit staff. Burt also made himself available during that time, and the staff always gathered around him, as he entertained them with stories of his life's adventures. Some camp directors would view Burt's nightly endeavor as an unnecessary expense, and even a waste of time. However, Burt built unprecedented loyalty by doing it this way. He would have the same coaches come back year after year, and the funny thing was, at the end of the week, some of those coaches enjoyed working the camp so much and appreciated how well Burt treated them that they donated their paychecks back to the Jets.

Burt also demonstrated his trust in the coaches by allowing them to let their guard down after they put the campers to bed at night. He had a saying that he always shared during the pre-camp staff meeting: "If you can hang—hang. If you can't hang—don't." It would always get a big laugh from the staff, but his simple words spoke volumes.

He didn't threaten the staff with ill-fated consequences of what would happen to them if they partied too much and were incapable of handling their camp coaching duties the next day. He didn't try to micromanage their lives. He just offered a casual reminder to the staff of their purpose and that they had a responsibility to the campers. In phrasing it in such a whimsical way, he conveyed his trust in his staff, and nobody wanted to let him down. His approach also made it easier for coaches to look out for each other and remind their colleagues to keep themselves in check.

Burt and his wife raised three daughters, each of whom turned out to be highly successful in her own right. As a parent, I always found Burt to be unusually trusting of his children. What started out as skepticism, however, turned into admiration. There would be times when I would see Burt's daughter's leaving the house for a night out to go clubbing, and I would ask him if that worried him. His response was simply, "No, they're good girls. I trust them."

He had the same response for far more daring incidents than his daughters heading out for a night on the town. Each of his daughters had, at a relatively young age, set out for adventures in less than tranquil environments. Right after she finished with her university studies, his eldest daughter traveled with Christian Aid to Northern India to work with awareness issues with the bottom ranks of the caste system.

His middle daughter, who holds a Master's degree from Oxford University, spent four weeks backpacking through southern China while still a university student. A few years later, she helped turn a dilapidated building in Ibanda, Uganda, into a secondary school where children could finish their education—a worthy endeavor, as a free state education is only provided up to the age of eleven in that poverty-stricken nation.

Burt's youngest daughter bravely hiked the Inca Trail in the Andes mountain range of Peru when she was just out of school, and despite her petite frame, she became a highly respected officer in the London Metropolitan Police Department.

His response—"*They're good girls. I trust them.*"—was a statement of Burt's confidence in his parenting. He was saying that he knew he raised them to make sound decisions. He exposed them to the right things and taught them the right lessons. Burt trusted in his parental abilities to instill values in his daughters. How many parents can do that? How many coaches can do that?

By making the simple nonchalant declaration that he trusted them, Burt empowered his daughters. They knew he had confidence in them, and that they had nothing to prove to him. That left them free to be themselves. He used trust to squelch the typical rebellious behavior and contentious relationship that often exists between a parent and their adolescent child.

Burt had a unique perspective on parenting in that his daughters weren't just his children; they were his friends. That is a far cry from the authoritarian parental model where parents command respect and make a conscious effort to keep a strict distance between them and their children. But think about it, isn't Burt's approach the perfect setup for healthy relationships based on mutual trust and concern? He didn't go out clubbing with his daughters or try to adopt the fashion of a younger genre, but he did speak to his daughters and treated them with the same level of trust and respect that he would have treated his closest friends. He wasn't raising a child; he was constructing a relationship with a future friend.

Friends have commonality, not exactness. Friends do not have to be fans of the same musician or television show, but they are aware of each other's likes and dislikes and are respectful of the differences. As children mature and grow to became adults, wouldn't it be ideal if they were able to feel as comfortable around their parents as they do their closest friends? It is an outside-the-box approach to behavior modification, but it works.

Burt's nontraditional way of looking at things found its way into his coaching. His atypical introduction to the sport of basketball could have partly caused that. Unlike most coaches who grew up playing and learning the game at a young age, Burt didn't become exposed to basketball until he was in his mid-20s.

In 1970, Burt traveled to America to work at The Greylock Camp for Boys in Becket, Massachusetts. The camp was founded in 1916 and sits on 300 acres of land in the Berkshire Mountains, about 2 hours west of Boston.[23] He came there to teach and coach soccer to aspiring campers, but it was another sport taught at the camp that caught his attention—basketball. At the end of the summer, Burt took a $50 bonus check home with him for winning all of the soccer games he coached. However, the fascination he had developed for basketball turned out to be much more impactful.

When he returned to England, his obsession with basketball grew. He started going to basketball coaching courses and studying everything he could get his hands on about the sport. After a while, he became skilled enough to be named an assistant coach of the Great Britain senior men's national team. In one of the greatest victories in British basketball history, Burt helped lead the team to a win over the Soviet Union team, who had only a few years' prior defeated the Americans and gone on to claim the gold medal in the 1988 Olympics.[24]

Burt was generous in revealing some of himself through stories of his personal life, which was another way he demonstrated trust to those serving under him. He was able to bond with others by doing that. He did not guard or worry about exposing his innermost thoughts, and because of this, the listener felt they were guardians of his past and possessed a genuine connection to him. Coincidentally, one of Burt's favorite stories involved a Russian basketball team.

He was coaching in an international tournament in Ireland and his team was set to go up against professional Russian powerhouse, Moscow Dynamo. Before the game, as usually is the custom in international play, coaches and players met at center court to exchange small gifts. The British coaches gave the usual pins and trinkets that teams traditionally exchange, but the economy was especially bad in Russia during this period, and the Dynamo players and coaches had no gifts to give in return.

Before leaving for the tournament, Burt had a friend ask him for a favor. His friend was looking to buy some *potcheen*—Irish moonshine made from potatoes—and had made arrangements for the delivery of a few bottles to Burt while in Ireland. All Burt had to do was bring them back home to England when he returned.

Potcheen, highly illegal at that time in Ireland, was typically produced by farmers in very rural parts of the countryside, not too different than the way moonshine is still produced in Appalachia today. Midway through the game with the Russians, a straggly looking character carrying a burlap sack walked up to Burt, who was on the sidelines coaching his team at that moment. The person introduced himself simply as "Jimmy" and handed Burt the glass bottles of potcheen.

Burt quickly got one of the team's managers to wrap the bottles in some towels and hide them until after the game. Later that night, Burt and another coach were back in their hotel room when an unexpected knock came at the door. It was the Russian coaches, and they were carrying two plastic hotel cups, a bottle of vodka, and a can of caviar. Although they spoke no English, they were doing their best to express their embarrassment and apologize for not having any gifts to exchange before the game.

Not completely sure what to do, Burt remembered the bottles of potcheen and decided to offer his guests a sampling of his cache. Potcheen is a clear liquid. To get the illegal alcohol past customs officials, it was often hidden in other bottles that would typically hold clear liquids. In this particular situation, *Jimmy* had disguised the potcheen in Bacardi rum bottles. When the Russian assistant coach saw the familiar label, he excitedly proclaimed, "Bacardi!" and proceeded to down a quick swig.

The potcheen hit him hard and sent him promptly to the sink to get a drink of water. He returned to utter one of the only English words he seemed to know, "*Another*." Despite Burt's best attempts to explain to him that it was not Bacardi, and to not chase his drink with water, the Russian coach repeated the sequence multiple times. The problem with potcheen is that water is believed to worsen the intoxicating effects because it mixes with the ethanol already in the person's system.[25] Burt claims he never saw that Russian coach again the rest of the tournament after he left the hotel room that night—not at the tournament banquet, not at any training sessions, not even at any games. His potcheen-induced disappearance remains a mystery.

I have many fond memories of my time with Burt, and I learned much from him. For years, I would return to England to

51

visit with him and work his camp. In yet another example of his trusting nature, he gave me full use of his car when the camp ended to travel throughout England. My wife and I drove countless miles exploring England and Scotland, and we even ventured into the rest of Europe on a few occasions. He never asked for a cent for using his car, never asked for my insurance information, and never told me to be careful. All he ever said was, "I trust you."

Arguably you can find truth in the belief that those who have much can afford to risk more and be more trusting. If their risk does not pay off, they can afford to cover the loss caused by the misbegotten trust. Perhaps. In Burt's case, he certainly was not an overtly wealthy man, but he didn't overextend his finances, and he was good at finding contentment in keeping things simple. He didn't over-indulge in expensive cars or houses. By not overextending his finances, he put himself in a position where he could, in fact, cover more losses and afford to be trusting.

That is good life advice, but it is also good coaching advice. Coaches can fall into the trap of overextending themselves, and that can put them in a compromising situation with their players. For instance, coaches can make too many promises to administrators, alumni, boosters, or even players that put them in a position where they feel they cannot afford to fail. They start to micromanage a player's every move. They start to turn a blind eye to potential disciplinary problems, particularly from the team's top players. They may even be tempted to break rules. In essence, they cannot afford to serve a higher purpose, nor assume the risks associated with trust.

This scenario creates an environment that abandons the importance of being a good teammate. Coaches are forced to prioritize something other than teaching players how to become good teammates.

Burt made quite an impression on me. I learned from him that it can sometimes be beneficial to drop your guard and allow yourself to be trusting of other people. Burt's approach to trust, and the generosity he showed me led directly to one of the core components of my definition of a good teammate.

4

GOOD TEAMMATES SHARE

WHEN my wife and I were first married, we bought a house that was within walking distance of a Little League baseball field. In the beginning, it was fantastic. I would walk to the park in the evenings and enjoy the atmosphere of the Little League experience—the smell of the concession stand, french fries, the resonance of the teams' dugout chants, and the sounds coming from the press box where one of the players' slightly older brother took on the game's public address duties. It was all so appealing and refreshing.

Sometimes, I would come home from my office exhausted from dealing with the usual campus politics and escape to those Little League games. I liked going to buy a hot dog from the concession stand and standing in line behind the uniformed little boy buying a snow cone, who moments earlier had been playing left field. That type of thing just doesn't happen at Major League ballparks.

Eventually, however, I became disgusted and stopped going to the Little League games. The more I watched them and got acclimated to the environment, the more I started to resent them. At first, it seemed like it was sports in its purest form. The kids were playing and having fun. But the longer I sat and watched the games and observed the unsettling things going on, I realized that Little League represented so much of what is wrong with amateur sports. It was a petri dish filled with the kind of vile contaminants that prevent the best life lessons from being learned through sports.

I routinely heard parents yell at umpires and coaches from the bleachers. I had no connection to the players on the field, nor the teams playing, and was watching as an impartial bystander. I often wondered if they would be as malcontent in front of their children if they saw the game with the same objectivity that I did.

I also wondered if they ever considered the message they sent the kids when they were so openly disrespectful to persons of authority. They not only set a poor example; they taught an ill-advised course of action for handling dissatisfaction. The seeds of bad habits were planted and nourished.

The coaching was deficient, which was not especially surprising. The coaches were all volunteers and seemed like nice enough people, but they were not experts in the field, and I don't think anybody expected them to be. While I respected their willingness to coach the kids, I found fault in what they emphasized. They were clearly coaching the kids to be competitive, but too frequently they missed out on an opportunity to teach more important things like sportsmanship and how to be a good teammate.

What bothered me more, though, was the readiness at which individuality was accepted and even promoted. Every player had their last name on the back of their uniform. Every player was equipped with the latest accessories. Every player had their own bat, and it was frowned upon to share that bat with another player. Sharing actually was discouraged! The players were not taught to embrace being a part of a team, and they were allowed to seek ways to differentiate themselves from the other members of their team.

At this level, sharing should have been encouraged and taught above all else. Sharing is a critical component of being a good teammate. Presumably, the kids each had their own bat based on the belief that something about that particular bat would give them an edge and improve their performance. That may have been true, but an opportunity to encourage sharing should not be overshadowed by an opportunity to improve performance, especially when the amount of potential improvement is minimal at this level. How much farther was the ball going to go when it was hit by that bat, compared to it being hit by any other bat on the market, when it was wielded by a Little Leaguer?

What was taught at that ball field, even if unintentional, was distancing the players from what pays the biggest dividends when that youngster moved into adulthood.

All three of the sentences used in the definition of a good teammate are interconnected. For instance, teammates who listen are showing they care by listening. Teammates who care about their team would share with their fellow teammates. And teammates who share are demonstrating that they listened to the needs of their teammates.

The time I spent in England with Burt was a great example of the value of sharing and how it benefits both the individual and the team. Burt shared generously, and he shared far more than just his possessions. That was the basis for me arriving at the conclusion that I need to include *good teammates share* in the definition. (In the catchphrase definition of a good teammate, I list caring ahead of sharing. I did that because I found it was easier for kids to remember that alphabetically, *caring* came before *sharing*. But chronologically, learning about sharing came first for me.)

Burt shared his possessions whenever he let me stay at his house, eat dinner with his family, and use his car to travel, but he shared far more than that—he shared his knowledge. Although he appreciated efficiency and was frugal with his time management, he always took the time to share with me what he had learned. Obviously, this happened in basketball when he taught things like shooting and defensive techniques, but it went beyond that.

For example, Burt was well traveled. One year, my wife and I had planned a trip to Rome, Italy after I was done working Burt's camp. As was typically the case, Burt had recommendations on sites to see and places to eat in Rome. He also advised me to watch my wallet, as pickpockets were rampant in the city. He mentioned that should I notice someone trying to pick my pocket, it was not wise to confront them physically, as persons in that line of work often carry knives. Confrontation can be very dangerous. Instead, he suggested I just yell and make loud noises. The last thing a pick-pocket wants is to have attention called to him.

Sure enough, a day or two into our trip, I was standing on a crowded subway car when I noticed what felt like someone fiddling with the zipper on my side pocket. I nonchalantly looked down and saw the hand of the man standing next to me inconspicuously slipping out of his coat sleeve and attempting to pick my pocket. I couldn't believe it! I started to panic, but then I remembered the advice Burt had shared with me about what to do if this situation should arise.

I let out an awkwardly loud and unintentionally high-pitched yelp. Everybody on the train turned and looked at me like I was crazy, but it worked. The pickpocket immediately distanced himself from me and quickly got off at the next stop. You can imagine how grateful I was for Burt's insight and how connected I felt to him when the dust settled on that incident.

To some degree, the dispensing of advice is a form of nostalgia. I suppose it is easier for the coach to share his knowledge with players, as it is often a necessity, and even his duty to do so. Far less common, however, is a player who shares what he has learned with his fellow teammates. Players are sometimes reluctant to do so because they are in competition with their teammates for playing time, respect, and the coach's attention. They don't want to risk losing any advantage they may have over the other players on the team. Good teammates don't think this way.

Good teammates are more concerned with the success of the team than they are with their individual success. This concern does not necessarily come naturally to younger players. I know it certainly didn't for me. As a kid, I was predisposed not to share "intellectual property" with others, including my siblings.

In our family, I was constantly pitted against my brothers and sisters. The comparisons were omnipresent. If I did poorly on a math test, I would hear, "Your brother never struggled in that class, why are you?" If my bedroom was messy, I would hear "Your sister keeps her room neat, why can't you?" It wasn't just to me that this happened, either. If I did something well, my siblings would undoubtedly be compared to me.

In time, the relentless comparisons caused us to become subconsciously resentful of one another. We built theoretical silos, filled with unshared knowledge that gave us a chance to get ahead of the others. I suppose my parents were trying to motivate us to do better. They did it so much that I am not even sure they realized they were doing it. It was their attempt at behavior modification. Maybe it worked. I know sometimes I yearned for their approval so much that I was motivated to tackle almost any task.

The problem, though, was it caused a division in our family, and our family was our team. I didn't want to see my siblings succeed. I loved them, but I knew if they got ahead, I would hear the comparisons.

This scenario plays out on sports teams, too, when coaches attempt to motivate players by willingly making comparisons between them and other members of the team. *Johnny was in the weight room working out this morning; why weren't you?* The obvious objective is to get the player in question to improve his skill set by increasing his strength.

The primary objective, however, is to increase the success of the team. If this player gets stronger, it is assumed that the team will achieve more success. Comparing him to Johnny, and challenging him to be more like his teammate, will not necessarily produce this desired result. Maybe the player comes in and lifts weights and does get stronger, but the resentment caused through the comparison can hurt the team's success and backfire in the long run.

Similar to what happened with me and my siblings, members of the team start to build their own silos and become reluctant to share knowledge, and ultimately, the spotlight with their teammates. This behavior is why it is important for coaches to be cautious of attempting to motivate their players by making comparisons. This can be hard to do.

To borrow a term usually associated with the art of meditation, a coach has a much better chance of promoting sharing and encouraging players to be good teammates if he or she can get the player to achieve a *quiet mind*. For players, this is a state of mind free from mental distractions and unwanted tension, like jockeying for the coach's approval and overcoming the comparisons made between them and their teammates.

Basic psychology, specifically Maslow's Hierarchy of Needs, supports this notion. Humans are motivated to achieve certain needs, and cannot advance to the next level without fulfilling the previous. A person who is drowning does not care about love. A person who is freezing does not care about financial security.

While I was discussing this book project with Burt, I had a conversation with his daughter Laura, in which she relayed to me a story her grandfather had told her about his POW experience. The Japanese had been extremely inhumane to the British soldiers and had all but starved them to death. Whenever the prisoners were finally liberated, they were cautioned not to eat too much and to eat very blandly until their bodies recovered. This was a tall order for a starving man.

When the ship carrying the freed prisoners back home to England stopped at an African port to refuel, one of the men couldn't contain himself and got off the ship to get something to eat. He overindulged in a big steak and died shortly after eating it. There are similar stories of this type of thing happening to concentration camp survivors. It is a condition known as *refeeding syndrome*.[26] The elder Burt conveyed to his granddaughter that when you are starving, you can't think of anything else but your hunger. You don't think logically. Your hunger consumes you.

Whenever players are starving for attention, they behave in a comparable way. They don't think rationally. They don't think about sharing and being a good teammate. Their basic needs have not been fulfilled to the point that they can rise to a position where they grasp the significance of being a good teammate.

Coaches would be hard pressed to see that every player's needs are completely satisfied. Not every distraction is within the coach's control. Some players have more baggage than others. But it is surely within the coach's means to bring them closer to a quieter *basketball* mind by eliminating open comparisons from his motivational repertoire. This is one of the things a coach can control.

Sharing is a crucial element of being a good teammate because it is a strong predictor of a person who is unselfish. I originally debated whether or not the word "unselfish" should be included in the definition of a good teammate. Being unselfish is an imperative quality of a good teammate. In the end, I decided against it.

Although the sentence "Good teammates are unselfish" is true, I wanted the definition to include action statements, not just descriptive words. A rather large number of adjectives, including unselfish, can be used to describe a good teammate, but there are a few action verbs that do a better job of this, than *share*. Good teammates take action and do things that others do not, and I wanted the definition to be reflective of this concept.

People who share are unselfish. And, people who are unselfish, share. Similarly, people who trust, share. And, people who share, trust.

I participated in an interesting activity a few years ago at the N.A.B.C. Coaches Convention. The presentation was given by a former Marine Corps Special Operations Officer named Eric Kapitulik, who founded a leadership development course called *The Program*.[27] During the presentation, Kapitulik posted a list of 34 values on the video screen. The list included things like passion, integrity, loyalty, and creativity.

He then gave us several minutes to narrow the list down to the ten words that we, individually, valued the most. After we got down to ten words, he gave us another minute to narrow it down to five words. This sequence repeated until the list was down to just one word, which was supposed to be the one value that we held in the highest regard.

It is an interesting exercise. It forces a person to confront their deepest feelings and identify their most cherished value. When I returned to campus, I did the same activity with my team and continued to do so for the next several seasons. I thought it would be good for the players to take a look at themselves and put some thought into what they valued. I also thought it would be beneficial for me to gain some insight into the players' psyche.

After a while, I decided it was just as important for a player to know his one word as it was for him to know the one word of each of the other players. A good teammate knows not only what motivates himself, but also what is important to his teammates and what motives them. This level of awareness gives a player a higher degree of understanding and leads to empathy. The activity became an exercise in sharing because the players had to share some of their innermost thoughts with each other.

I run a relatively popular kid's basketball camp every summer. With the continued growth of AAU and youth travel teams, summer camps have become a dying breed. I hear sad stories all the time about how camp enrollments are down and how camps that have been in existence for decades are folding because of dwindling attendance. That hasn't been the case with my summer camp because, quite to the contrary, it continues to grow every year.

This past summer, we had 380 kids at our Mount Aloysius camp. To put that number in context, consider that our camp is not located in a particularly strategic nor convenient location. The campus is quite some distance from any real population concentrations, and we are also in competition with several other conceivably more appealing camps, including a neighboring NCAA Division I camp.

Our facilities are certainly not a contributing factor to our camp's popularity, either, since we typically have to set up temporary courts in parking lots, and other areas, with lower quality portable hoops. With all of this, I suspect the attractiveness of our camp stems from what we teach and accentuate during the week.

I enjoyed traveling to England and working Burt's camp. Some of the structure of my camp is based on Burt's camp. What I feel is unique about our camp, however, is the amount of emphasis we place on having fun and recognizing good teammates. In fact, the highlight of the camp is the all-star game. Our all-star game, however, is not comprised of the best players in camp but the best teammates in camp.

At the beginning of the week, I gather the entire camp together and tell them what I expect from them. I then explain about the all-star game, and I tell them what the staff is looking for in selecting players to participate in the all-star game. It is made clear to them that the all-star team will not necessarily include the best players, but it will absolutely include the best teammates. Everyone has a chance to make the all-star team, regardless of their size or their current basketball skill level. This is where I first go over the definition of a good teammate.

I tell them that the coaches are always watching, and that we are looking for kids who care, share, and listen in their games, during drills and stations, and even at lunch. Every day, I take a few minutes to expand on each of those topics during our lecture time. Whenever I cover sharing, I make sure to explain to them that they can share on the court by passing to their teammates and not being a ball hog. They can share the credit by pointing at a teammate who gave them a nice assist. They can share their enthusiasm by giving their teammates high fives. Of course, I also explain that there are other ways off the court to show they share.

For example, they can help clean up the cafeteria after the campers are done with lunch. Taking pride in the cleanliness of the campus cafeteria shows they care, but it is also a way to demonstrate sharing, by sharing the workload with the housekeepers and maintenance staff.

I am amazed at how clean the cafeteria is when the campers are done with lunch, considering how many kids ate there. I see several kids picking up candy wrappers, wiping up spilled drinks, and pushing in chairs. They are cleaning up messes that they didn't even make. It is an impressive feat to get kids to respond in this manner.

Helping with the cleanup also gets the kids to see themselves as a part of multiple teams. Sure they play for the Bulls or the Lakers or the Tar Heels, or whatever camp team they were placed on for the week. But as a camper, they are part of the entire camp, and everyone in camp is on *the* team. Whenever they clean up the cafeteria, the entire camp team looks good. The cafeteria workers are complimentary. The housekeeping and maintenance staffs are appreciative. We all benefit from cleaning up the cafeteria when we are done.

To take it a step further, while the kids are on campus during the week of camp, they learn that they are also part of the campus team. The housekeepers and maintenance staff become their teammates. They are taught to appreciate the relationship and not take it for granted. They come to understand that they really are sharing in the workload and the responsibility to keep the campus looking nice. Moreover, they learn to share their most valuable commodity—their time. It takes time to stay behind and help tidy up the cafeteria. They can choose to spend that time any way they want, and they choose to share it with others and on something that is beneficial to their team.

When it comes to the actual all-star game at the end of the week, I do my best to make it a special occasion. We play loud, upbeat music during the game, turn the regular lights down, and use the flashing colored lights. It is rock 'n roll basketball and a party-like atmosphere. I want the efforts of those kids who made the all-star team to be recognized and rewarded. Special occasions like birthdays, holidays, and other life achievements are celebrated with parties, and this accomplishment should be handled no differently. The members of the all-star teams get popsicles and are given special neon colored t-shirts with the words "certified good teammate" printed on the front and our definition of a good teammate printed on the back.

We routinely see kids in the all-star game who haven't scored a single basket the whole camp. We see kids who are too short and too slow. We see kids who were the first to be eliminated in nearly every contest or drill we did. Somehow they all figured out that you don't have to be the most athletically gifted player to be a good teammate. All it takes is a little self-sacrifice and enthusiasm for going the extra mile.

Sometimes, though, we do see the best players, leading scorers, and most skilled players make the all-star game. But they didn't make it based on their athletic ability; they made it because of their ability to be a good teammate. The two entities are not necessarily at odds. The best players can also be the best teammates. I would argue that a coach's definition of *best* player is lacking, if it doesn't include being a good teammate.

I didn't always do our camp all-star game like this. I used to run it like a traditional all-star game—and it was usually a problematic endeavor. I would undoubtedly get a telephone call from a parent complaining about their child not making the all-star game. Whenever we played the game, there would be disgruntled players who felt that they should have been put on the all-star team, pouting on the sidelines and refusing to cheer for the players who did.

Once I changed the criteria for the all-star game, all of those problems went away. One of the best parts of the all-star game now is the way the other campers cheer for the kids who are playing in the games. It really is electric and immensely gratifying. Duke's Cameron Crazies have nothing on our campers cheering during the all-star game. The reason for the enthusiasm is because everyone who made the all-star game is worthy of being there. These are all the kids that the other kids like being around. Sure, they may sometimes be a little quirky or undertalented, but they are likeable. The other kids and parents simply cannot argue with the selections.

By modifying the criteria for the all-star game, I also de-emphasized the machismo and vanity that historically accompanies these types of games. Instead, we made it about something practical that can be applied to the real world—being a good teammate.

Coincidently, if I were the CEO of a Fortune 500 company, or a corporate headhunter, I would quickly gobble up the kids who make our camp all-star teams. I would offer them employment right now and worry later about what specific job they would eventually do because these kids are talented and already understand what it means to be a team player. They will most assuredly be assets to any company that employs them.

* * *

Al Robinson, an Associated Press reporter from Pittsburgh, wrote a story about my overseas experience and the season I spent with Burt. The unique nature of the story piqued the interest of several college coaches, but it did not yield any immediate Division I offers. I improved considerably as a result of my year with Burt, but I still had not grown to be a legitimate prospect for college basketball's highest level. This left me searching for yet another route to reach my goal of playing in the March Madness tournament.

One of the Division I coaches who had contacted me as a result of the article proposed an alternative for me to attend a junior college he recommended. He made an appointment for me to meet Dennis Gibson, the head coach at Garrett College, in Deep Creek Lake, Maryland. It was an introduction that would become abundantly important to my development as a coach.

I would go on to spend three years playing for Gibson at Garrett. Sandwiched between two of my favorite years of playing the sport of basketball would be a medical redshirt year, resulting from a torn anterior cruciate ligament in my knee that required reconstructive surgery. I didn't think of it at the time, but the years I spent at Garrett set me up to one day become a coach—a direct result of the admiration I developed for Gibson, and the amount of trust he built with me.

Burt showed me how to trust and how to share. Gibson would show me how to *build* trust and how to care. And there is a difference.

5

GARRETT COUNTY'S FINEST— THE THIRD FACE ON MY MOUNT RUSHMORE

CONDUCTING a job interview is an acquired skill. It can be difficult to see beyond the otherwise impressive façade that some people erect during the interview process. Skilled interviewees are often able to present themselves as everything the interviewer wants them to be, masking their true self. I have found that one way to crack the façade is to ask, "If they made a movie about you, who would play you?" and allow them an opportunity to at least expose how they view themselves. Their answers can be incredibly insightful.

For instance, if they answer "myself," then you are clearly in the midst of a genuine narcissist. If they refuse to answer or brush the question off with a casual "I don't know," then they are hiding something they don't want to expose to you. If they answer with the name of an actor or actress who bears a similarity to how they look, then you know they value physical appearance. If they answer with the name of an actor or actress who has a specific disposition, then you know they place a premium on personality. If, however, their selection is reflective of both their physical appearance and their personality, then they probably have a good sense of self-awareness and are comfortable in their skin.

This can also be a worthwhile exercise in gaining perspective on how others see you. In that regard, if they made a movie about the life of Dennis Gibson, then Clint Eastwood would undoubtedly play him. When I first met Gibson, a younger *Dirty Harry* or *The Outlaw Josey Wales* Clint Eastwood would have been cast for the part. As he has aged, a *Gran Torino* or *Million Dollar Baby* Clint Eastwood would still probably get the role.

Beyond the obvious physical similarities, Gibson—the third person on my Mount Rushmore—shares many of the same gritty personality traits that have turned Clint Eastwood's portrayals over the years into some of America's most beloved characters. Beneath the squinted-eyes, scowl-faced, tough-guy exterior is a clever and otherwise charming individual. Beneath that layer is a caring man with a soft spot for the disadvantaged underdog.

When it comes to building trust, Dennis Gibson is an excellent example of how to do it successfully. His primary method of building trust is by showing he cares. For the better part of the last 40 years, Gibson has been in one way or another associated with the Garrett College men's basketball team—first as a player, then as an assistant coach, and eventually as head coach and athletic director.

The college is nestled in the Allegheny Mountains of western Maryland, a region renowned for its outdoor recreational opportunities. With activities like sailing, kayaking, and canoeing in the summer, and skiing, snowboarding, and ice fishing in the winter, Garrett County and the Deep Creek Lake area have long been the playground for the adventuresome spirit and the get-away locale for vacationing urbanites from Baltimore, Washington, D.C., and Pittsburgh. Located within this holiday retreat, however, is one of the nation's most successful junior college basketball programs.

As the head coach of the Garrett College Lakers, Dennis Gibson has amassed over 600 career wins, averaging nearly 20 wins per season for his career. He has captured multiple titles during his tenure and has produced numerous NJCAA All-Americans. In all his time at the Garrett helm, he has only ever had one losing season. As might be expected with that kind of longevity, it is his legacy of off-court victories that is the most noteworthy.

The experience of leaving England and enrolling at Garrett Community College, as it was then known, turned out to be more beneficial than I ever expected. I thought I was just getting an opportunity to showcase my improved skills and gain some much-desired exposure. I was naïve enough to think it would be a brief speed bump on the path leading to my dream. Looking back, I was incredibly delusional about my talents as a player. In the end, that didn't matter, as I got the chance to play under the tutelage of another outstanding coach.

Much like Burt, Gibson was tough and could be very blunt at times. However, the longer I played for him, the easier it was for me to see past that. It's been 20 years since I first put on a Garrett uniform, and I am still learning from Gibson to this day. In truth, the myriad of things I learned while I was playing for him pales in comparison to everything I have learned from him as our relationship has evolved since the end of my playing days.

Whenever any new coach assumes the reins of his first team, he thinks he is ready to handle whatever comes his way. I was no exception. No matter how well you think you know the game, there are some things you have to deal with that you are ill-equipped to manage and that you don't anticipate, like discipline problems and navigating the politics of academia. Gibson became my sounding board. He helped me understand how to operate as a coach without losing my sanity.

Coaching at Garrett College is not an easy gig. It is a very challenging endeavor for many reasons. Beyond the limited resources and less than advantageous rural location, there are always the issues of time and, for lack of a better term, "clientele" that come with junior college athletics. Players who end up at this level always have a flaw. Sometimes, as it was in my case, it is a shortcoming in the form of athletic ability. Other times, it is an academic issue or a matter of some social deficiency. In JUCO, you see it all as a coach.

Problems with players—and problem players—are the norm. Inevitably, the coach will handle several issues during the season. For most teams, the expected response would be to kick the player off the team, but in JUCO, you can't always do that. If you followed that course of action, there soon wouldn't be any players left to coach. And it's not like high school, where there is continually a younger class of players coming up from the feeder system. JUCO coaches have to be savvy in handling their players. The fact that in all of his years as a head coach at Garrett, Gibson has only ever kicked two players off the team during the season speaks volumes about his coaching abilities and his capacity to manage at-risk players.

A few years ago, *Basketball Times* did a feature on Garrett and labeled Gibson as the coach of one of the "most unheralded (junior college) programs in the U.S.A." The article described in detail the challenges of coaching at the small school, and it highlighted the point that "the majority of players at Garrett are there because they have been thwarted by other schools." The article quoted Gibson as saying, "I take projects, rejects or under-recruited players."[28]

The matter of him taking those types of players is important, but what he does with them and how he does it is impressive.

Perhaps the biggest problem for JUCO coaches is the issue of time. Every player at that level is looking to move on to a higher and more prestigious four-year program, and they want it to happen as quickly as possible. That translates into JUCO coaches having a very limited amount of time to build a relationship with their players. This is typically two years, and in some cases, even less. Of course, the cornerstone to building a relationship is building trust. Under accelerated circumstances, Gibson has been able to do this on a consistent basis.

A quick Google search for "leadership books" produces over 175 million results. There is no shortage of information on the topic. Most of the books contain advice on the value of leaders making a personal connection with their subordinates. Suave leaders are very skilled at doing this. Small talk with their workers is a deliberately sought exercise. The best are even able to remember the most minute details of a previous conversation, like the name of their subordinate's pet or the illness that has afflicted the subordinate's great aunt. Over time, making these types of connections pays dividends, as does the practice of sending short notes or giving small, unexpected gifts.

Politicians often take advantage of the effectiveness of this approach. My neighbor once communicated to me how impressed he was to receive a congratulatory note in the mail accompanied by the newspaper clipping of his son's name listed on the school's honor roll list. Our local state congressman had sent it to him. It was such a small gesture to build loyalty, but an effective one nonetheless.

The obvious key is that these tactics work over time. Gibson doesn't exactly have that luxury of time, yet he still engages in similar practices. The difference, however, is that Gibson's actions display genuineness. The reality is that the politician did not take the time to comb through the newspapers and seek out my neighbor's mailing address. More than likely that task was assigned to an intern. The politician was not really proud of the honor roll listing, he just wanted my neighbor's loyalty—and his vote.

Gibson doesn't operate like that. He wouldn't ask a player in passing how his girlfriend was doing just because some leadership strategist advised him that there is value to doing that. If he makes the effort to ask a player about his girlfriend, then it is because he is genuinely interested and he cares to know the answer. He does not engage in glorified small talk. Players can spot this right away.

When I was in high school, I had a football coach who would walk the field whenever we were in our pre-game stretching lines, shaking the hand of every player on the team and offering a few words of seemingly personalized encouragement. I loved how this attention used to make me feel and looked forward to it immensely every game. It made me feel special.

But then one game, the coach got sidetracked by something and forgot which row he had just completed and ended up walking down a line of previously spoken to players. As he shook hands, I noticed he repeated the same things to those players that he had moments earlier said to me. Suddenly, it didn't feel so personalized and sincere. From then on, I still liked it when that coach walked through the stretching lines, but it never felt as genuine as it did before his snafu.

In the winter months, Garrett County gets snow—a lot of snow. During my freshman season, we got 213 inches.[29] That is almost 18 *feet* of snow! By comparison, that same year Buffalo, New York, a city notorious for its snow accumulation, got a mere 141 inches. Over the last decade, Garrett has averaged 166 inches of snow annually.[30] Fargo, North Dakota has an annual average of 52 inches, while Anchorage, Alaska has only a 75-inch average.[31]

The National Weather Service theorizes Garrett's high snow-fall totals to be the result of its elevation and odd location, suscep-tible to both nor'easter storms and lake effect snow.[32] The county is also predisposed to a rare phenomenon known as up-slope snow, where moisture from the valley rises up the mountainside.[33] What-ever the reasons, that kind of snowfall can be problematic, and has the potential to wreak havoc on a basketball season.

I lived in an off-campus apartment my first year at Garrett. At one point during the season, the snow had fallen so fast and piled up so high that my roommate and I were stuck in our place. All of our cars were snowbound. After spending several days cooped up in our apartment, we were finally able to shovel a narrow quar-ter-mile path through the waist-high snow out to the main road. I didn't think we were going to ever get our cars out, though. One day, out of nowhere, Gibson showed up in a truck with our assis-tant coach Dave Martin and plowed us out.

He didn't have to do that. Nobody asked him to do it, and cer-tainly no one expected him to do it. Showing up with that plow was done out of the goodness of his heart, and there were no strings attached to his actions.

It was not like he sat in his office and convinced himself that he should go bail out those kids because they will play harder for him and rebound better in the next game. Those thoughts never crossed his mind. His gesture was because he cared about us. He knew we needed help, and he was in a position to help. A person willing to selflessly help another is a person worthy of trust.

There are countless other examples of Gibson doing similar things for players. For instance, sometimes the college's cafeteria would shut down, and the snow would prevent players from leav-ing the dorms to get off campus and get something to eat. When those occasions occurred, Gibson and his wife would inevitably send home-cooked soup or pasta to the dorms for the players to eat. Again, he wasn't trying to make a connection; it was because he cared.

Similar to Burt, Gibson had a less-than-conventional basketball background, and I suspect that background played a large part in his perspective on players and why he cared about them.

Despite being six-foot-seven, Gibson never played high school basketball. He tried out for the school's basketball team in eighth grade, but he got cut. The experience left a bad taste in his mouth, and his self-confessed stubbornness made him unreceptive to any high school coach's invitation to come out for a team after that.

His family owned a store just outside of town, and Gibson spent the bulk of his high school years working in the family business. When his father died during his freshman year of high school, Gibson felt obliged to spend even more time working at the family store. The hours he spent laboring in the family business were clearly the root of his work ethic, but not necessarily his basketball aptitude.

Garrett County had recently broken ground on a community college and had announced plans to start a basketball team the year following Gibson's graduation from high school. While playing in a recreation league that summer with some friends, Gibson was approached by Garrett's newly hired men's basketball coach and asked to consider joining the team.

The timing seemed right, and Gibson decided to give it a try. But there was one catch: so many others had also been asked to come out for the team that they had to hold tryouts. They didn't have enough uniforms for everybody. Flashbacks to his previous basketball tryout experience flared up whenever the coaches announced that they could not pick which player should receive the final roster spot. Much to Gibson's chagrin, they chose an unusual method to make their choice.

He and another player battled it out in a game of one-on-one in front of everyone for the last remaining slot on Garrett's roster. This time, Gibson emerged as the victor, and his relationship with Garrett College basketball officially commenced. Ironically, the player who he beat went on to become a successful businessman and sponsored Gibson's tip-off tournament at Garrett for many years. I guess it was safe to say there were no hard feelings.

After a successful two years on Garrett's team, Gibson transferred to Bridgewater College in Virginia. He chose Bridgewater because two of his friends from high school were already heading there. Unfortunately, both of those friends withdrew from Bridgewater shortly after he arrived. Gibson stuck around long enough to make an impact on the school's basketball team, but he was not able to finish his degree at Bridgewater. After his father's passing and his departure for Bridgewater, Gibson's mother struggled to manage the family business. He moved back home to help alleviate the burden and eventually finished his degree at nearby West Virginia University.

While back home, a friend saw an advertisement in *The Washington Post* for an open tryout for the Baltimore Metros in the Continental Basketball League (CBA). The CBA was America's foremost semi-professional basketball league and feeder system to the more prominent National Basketball Association. The friend convinced Gibson to go to the tryout. Over one hundred legitimate players attended the first date of the tryout, with more arriving every day. Many of them already had prior NBA experience, having spent at least the previous season with the likes of the Boston Celtics or the Philadelphia 76ers.

Former NBA and ABA All-Star Larry Cannon coached the team. A Big 5 Hall of Fame inductee at La Salle University, Cannon was a *Parade* All-American at Philadelphia's Lincoln High, where he averaged 35.2 points per game. Only the great Wilt Chamberlain averaged more points in a season (47.5 in Philadelphia Public League play).[34]

In what is tantamount to one of the great American rags-to-riches basketball stories, Gibson, who never even played high school ball, was signed by the Metros. When his stint in the CBA ended, Gibson returned to Garrett, where he served as an assistant coach at his alma mater, until he was named the head coach in 1985.

The unusual nature of his ascension through the basketball world played a role in how he viewed players, and why he cared about them so much. He was not predisposed to how coaches are supposed to interact with players, nor was he jaded by traditional coaching methodology. He cared about players' well-being because that is how you are supposed to treat your fellow man. To Gibson, it was as simple as that.

He built trust with the players because they knew that he cared about their needs as a person. He also cared whether or not they produced on the court. There was not necessarily a connection between the two, either. Gibson was able to separate the player on the court from the person off of the court better than anyone I have ever seen.

By concerning himself with the results the player produced on the court, he made it clear that politics, favorites, or past reputation played no part in who got playing time. By concerning himself with the well-being of the player off the court, he also made it clear that he cared about the leading scorer no more than he cared about the worst player on the team. That is one of the primary reasons players came to willingly trust him. They knew he cared about his players but likewise knew that anyone who produced would get court time.

In general, people remember acts of kindness done for them, especially when the person doing it doesn't have anything to gain from the act. This builds genuine trust and loyalty into the relationship. One time, my maternal grandfather was eating in a restaurant when he experienced an unexpected gesture of appreciation from someone he had once helped.

My mother's father, Earl Hinzman, was an interesting man. He started teaching all twelve grades in a one-room schoolhouse and eventually retired as the acting superintendent of Marion County Schools in West Virginia. At some point during his teaching career, he was the principal at an elementary school. There was a boy in the school whose family was struggling on many levels. Among other things, the boy was badly in need of a haircut. My grandfather took him to a barber and paid for his haircut. I'm sure my grandfather had never thought about the occasion again. Fast forward over 50 years later, and the same boy secretly paid for my grandfather's meal as a token of his appreciation.

My grandfather's health had deteriorated significantly by this point in time. Skin cancer had eroded his face in his twilight years, and he was confined to a wheelchair. The boy, who had apparently gone on to have a very successful and lucrative life, still recognized the man who had once extended the small act of kindness toward him so many years prior. In a note he had left with the waitress, the "boy" recalled the story, sharing that he had never forgotten the kind deed, and cited the occurrence as a defining moment in his life. That haircut gave the youngster a new level of self-confidence that he most certainly needed.

I foresee many similar incidents in Gibson's future, as he has performed countless deeds of a comparable nature over the years for needy players. The restaurant story could have just as easily been about him. The only unfortunate difference is that too-restrictive collegiate rules often limited the types of help he could sometimes provide. In the shadow of big time/big budget college sports, over-regulation is a sad byproduct of rule-making administrators who have become out of touch with life in the small college trenches.

Beyond the off-court gestures, Gibson employed a few other means to build trust with his players, including the infusion of his family with the team. It was subtle at times, but it was never contrived and always genuine.

His wife, daughter, and two sons have for years been mainstays in the Garrett fan section. Both of Gibson's sons eventually played for him at Garrett. In fact, they finished their careers among the program's most successful players. Long before that, they were just the coach's kids, who liked to ride the team bus to away games and hang out at practice.

As a former Garrett player, I vividly remember his family spending time around the team. It was small, and often unspoken, but seeing his wife in the stands at games meant something to all of us. She attended the games with religious devotion. It also meant something to us to have his kids at practices and other team functions. The three of them were still in elementary school when

I played. There were many times when we would be at practice or working out in the gym, and they would be playing with their toys on the sidelines. Sometimes Gibson would walk out of the gym and leave only the players to keep an eye on the kids.

Whenever this happened, it was hard not to feel a sense of ownership of the kids, much the way a big brother would for a younger sibling. What a sense of responsibility, to be entrusted with the coach's most prized possessions. Everyone values family and Gibson was no exception. He build trust by allowing us to connect with his family. We knew the premium he placed on family and how important they were to him. We could appreciate the potential vulnerability that must have existed in exposing them to us.

Beyond the trust he built by having his family around the players, he also provided us with superb parental modeling. Coaches, and persons of authority in general, rarely allow their subordinates a glimpse of themselves outside the boundaries of the office and their leadership position. They establish empathy when they allow that glimpse. It is like seeing an animal in its natural habitat, which always leaves a more memorable impression than seeing the animal in captivity. The player sees the coach in a different light when this happens.

Obviously, a reasonable balance must certainly be struck in how much a leader exposes of himself. Gibson seemed always to know the right amount of distance to keep from the players on his teams. As players moved on and left Garrett, that distance often became proportionately less. It was not uncommon for former players to stop back and visit him. Whenever they did, it was clear that the relationship was different, more relaxed. As a player who witnessed this firsthand, it was reassuring to see how other players who had traveled the path before me clearly trusted him and enjoyed his company. Seeing that behavior built added trust in him.

The link between longevity and trust is undeniable. Consumers gravitate towards companies that have been in existence for generations. It is because they trust them. Investors look for the same type of companies to financially back for similar reasons. They have a proven record.

Gibson's high number of career wins and the championships he's won demonstrate competence, a crucial element to trust, but the three decades he has coached at Garrett may go even further in building it.

In his book *The Mentor Leader*, Tony Dungy quotes his former Pittsburgh Steelers boss and coach Chuck Noll as saying, "The Mercenaries will always defeat the draftees, but the volunteers will crush them both."[35] This statement has relevance to the current landscape of the coaching profession, particularly related to the issue of trust.

The sports world has become laden with *mercenary coaches*. They don't care for whom they coach, as long as the pay is there. They bounce from team to team and from school to school. I understand to a degree where they are coming from, and it is hard to find fault in a person who wants to better their financial standing by taking a higher paying job. But that is not the point. In reality, there are numerous legitimate reasons for coaches taking other jobs. My concern, however, is with the effect the coaching carousel has on the players.

Naturally, the matter of trust will be called into question as long as coaches jump from job to job. Players are instinctively skeptical of a coach if they think the coach's motives are less than pure, like always looking for his next job. Gibson has had opportunities to move on to other jobs during his career, but by staying at Garrett for so long, he in essence became a volunteer coach. That label has nothing to do with the amount of his paycheck, but rather with the clarity of his motivation to coach. He was at Garrett because he wanted to be there. It was his choice.

The consistency he brought to his position by staying in the same place gave the players reason to trust him. He was consistent. He wasn't going anywhere. He wasn't going to abandon them.

When the sun sets on his coaching career, I don't know if Gibson will have any regrets that he coached at the same school for so long. But I can say with absolute certainty that his doing so was appreciated by his players—and it built trust. It made a difference in many of our lives.

6

GOOD TEAMMATES CARE

CARING is the most desirable quality of a good teammate because it is the impetus for the many other defining characteristics. People who care are willing to do nearly anything to ensure the success and preservation of something that is important to them. Hall of Fame football coach Lou Holtz is often recognized for saying, "If enough people care, we can solve anything in this world."[36] The challenge for coaches and leaders is to find a way to get enough people on their team to care.

In most cases, getting an individual to care about something other than his or her immediate interests becomes a matter of establishing pride. What are you proud of? What are you proud enough of to invest your energy in protecting?

Good teammates take pride in all facets of their team, not just what directly benefits them. Taking pride in something is another way of showing you care. Much like I chose the action verb *share* over the adjective *unselfish*, I chose *care* over *pride* to use in the definition of a good teammate. Pride, however, may be an easier way to describe and understand why good teammates should care.

My wife and daughters are huge fans of all things Disney. Disney toys, books, movies, and a variety of other Mickey Mouse-inspired paraphernalia fill our house. Naturally, our family's favorite vacation spot has become Orlando's Walt Disney World.

Regarding getting teammates to care, perhaps nobody does it better than Disney management.

The park is always clean and pristine, something that was of supreme importance to founder, Walt Disney. There are stories of Walt routinely walking through the park and picking up trash that he happened to notice laying along the sidewalk. He didn't summon the maintenance staff or say anything to them at all. He took so much pride in the cleanliness of his park that he set whatever ego he was entitled to aside and picked up the trash himself.

In this regard, Dennis Gibson shared Walt Disney's capacity to set aside his ego and to pick up the proverbial trash. Countless times I've seen Gibson sweep the floor, wash uniforms, and set up the popcorn machine. Both Gibson and Walt Disney set a standard of caring for those under their command. In Disney's case, this standard is still present, long after his death.

The popularity of Disney World has, not surprisingly, led to long waiting lines for many of the most prominent attractions. Whenever our family is stuck in one of those lines, I like to people-watch. I am particularly fascinated by the park employees whom Disney management refers to as "cast members." They seem to take the same kind of pride in keeping the park clean as Walt Disney did. I see random cast members picking up stray trash all the time. They are not just maintenance employees assigned to do the task, either. I see ride operators and retail vendors picking up trash too. That is the degree of pride they have for the park.

At the Disney Institute, a consulting wing of the company that specializes in sharing the Disney methodology with businesses seeking to incorporate its successful practices, they refer to this as "values-infused" leadership.[37] The funny thing about this phenomenon is that it frequently snowballs, with subsequently hired employees mimicking the prideful actions of the veteran employees. I can speak from personal experience as a Disney World customer. I, too, feel compelled to wipe off my tables and pick up trash whenever I'm in the park. I know I am not alone in feeling this way, as I have also seen other customers do this.

During one of our Disney trips, my youngest daughter was eating a chocolate-covered Mickey Mouse ice cream bar. It was a typical hot summer day in Florida, and the ice cream was melting at a faster rate than her little mouth could handle. A big chunk of the bar melted away and went crashing to the sidewalk. I started to wipe off her hands and face, but before I could clean the ice cream that had fallen on the ground, a cast member arrived to take care of it.

Expeditiously, he swept up the mess and then took a rag from his pocket to get the remaining chocolate residue off the pavement. When he finished, he looked up at my daughter and smiled and then offered the seemingly standard Disney cast member greeting to all little girls, "Hello, princess."

I was grateful for the cast member's hospitable response. I didn't necessarily feel embarrassed by the incident, but I did kind of feel guilty. I like going to Disney, seeing the cleanliness, and feeling a sense of pride in doing my part to keep it clean. Disney pride is so amazingly abundant that it triggers feelings of guilt in its guests over something like that.

Disney does have other measures in place to help keep up the immaculate appearance of its properties. For example, they have trash cans placed every 27 paces in the parks, which is the average distance the company estimates a visitor holds onto a candy wrapper before getting rid of it.[38] Beyond just a commitment to cleanliness, this is also a testament to the amount of time and effort Disney invests in studying its customers and the attention it pays to detail.

Paying attention to detail can go a long way to establishing competency, which leads to trust. People want to follow leaders who have experience and know what they are talking about. At the same time, attention to detail can potentially jeopardize the building of trust, especially when it falls into the category of micromanagement—a leadership term that often has a negative connotation.

The typical perception is that micromanagement is an inefficient way to lead. It can stymy creativity and lead to disengagement. The biggest problem with micromanagement, though, is that it destroys trust—a necessary component of solid relationships. People who are micromanaged usually feel that management has a lack of faith in them. From a management perspective, however, I understand the origins of micromanagement.

There is pressure on the manager to achieve. Maybe the pressure is coming from outside sources; maybe it is self-imposed. In either case, it is the manager's money, reputation, and more that is at stake. The manager who finds himself in this position puts considerable effort into ensuring that all aspects of the operation run at peak level. There is little room for chance, and that is why he is so involved.

If they can get this person to stop taking shortcuts, maybe they can get him to be more thorough in his work. If they can get that person to take a few more shortcuts, maybe they can get him to be more efficient. They hover over shoulders in the hopes of maximizing output and thereby generating success. It is hard to find fault with the micromanager's intention because this method often produces results—temporarily.

Micromanagement is not the most effective way to lead, nor is it the most effective way to coach. Teams that are micromanaged only know how to do what they are told. They become drone-like and unable to think and act on their own. When applied to the real world, this is not a skill set that leads to prolonged success and happiness. Coaches who micromanage their players set them up for failure later in life. Micromanagement sets in motion a culture of compliance instead of a culture of commitment.

The most successful businesses—and teams—have a culture of commitment, where the team members care about the well-being of the team and are committed to its continued improvement. Employees only doing as they are told does not lead to growth. It creates a situation where teams are constantly fighting to maintain the status quo. This will catch up with them in time.

Economies change. Industries evolve. Innovation happens. As the classic business analogy goes, at some point in history there were a lot of extremely successful bullwhip manufacturers. The advent of the automobile and mass transportation negated the demand for that industry. The most prosperous organizations are constantly growing, which reinforces another business axiom: *You're either growing, or you're dying.*

Disney is a living example of this. Look how much it continues to grow and expand each year. The origins of this growth can certainly be attributed at least in some part to the commitment of its employees. Commitment is another defining element of caring.

Committed teammates, who by nature care, can be trusted. They become an extension of the principle leader and can be trusted to function in tune with the leader. There is no need to micromanage that kind of employee. They are fighting for the same things as the leader, and their motives are clear. It is less risky to give them a heightened level of freedom than to micromanage them.

In many ways, building trust with members of the team is the start of getting them to care about the team's standards and the team's values.

Everything about Disney is wholesome. Their reputation for promoting family values is universally understood. I like having players come by my office and hang out during the day. But several years ago, I was having an issue with them engaging in entirely inappropriate language and behavior when they visited, the kind that is characteristically labeled as "locker room" talk.

I was hearing too much cursing and stories about co-eds that I felt like I was hanging out down at the docks with a bunch of sailors. To combat this, I started referring to the door that is used to enter my office as a "Disney" door. That meant that if it couldn't be said or done in a Disney movie, then it shouldn't be said or done—or even thought—inside of that door.

It was a lighthearted solution to what could become a very serious problem. Every player understands this message and what Disney represents. I would probably have stopped the cursing and inappropriate storytelling if I had come down hard on them and just aggressively chewed them out when it happened. But drawing that kind of hard line and demanding they adhere to yet another rule, the intention of which they may not even fully appreciate, would have only gotten them to be compliant for the short term. They would have still talked that way; they just wouldn't have talked that way in front of me.

The Disney door approach, on the other hand, got them involved in the problem. It gave them something easy to remember and to which they could relate. Eventually, the Disney door standard expanded to include other settings than just my office. The players started to use the Disney expression around each other. I wasn't ready to condone the players speaking inappropriately in any setting, but I was also realistic about typical *boys-will-be-boys* behavior.

Introducing the Disney door kept me from nagging the players, and it brought about a drastic reduction to their impropriety. Moreover, it made them cognizant of the issue without being defensive. This is exactly how a teammate who cares is supposed to respond to a team problem.

If a coach is going to get a player to become a good teammate, then the coach must look for creative ways to get players to stop thinking about their rights and privileges. He must instead get them to think about their obligations and responsibilities.

On another occasion, I was starting to have an issue with scratches on our team's locker room door. It sounds like such a trivial problem, but I want our locker room to feel like a sanctuary for our players. I try to emphasize how important it is to keep it clean and respect the luxury we enjoy in having our space.

The problem revolved around the main entry door to the locker room. We keep our basketballs stored on a cart inside the locker room. The first player to get dressed rolls the cart out to the court. The last player to leave the court after practice pushes the cart back into the locker room. The ball cart has a metal frame. Whenever the player would push the cart back into the locker room, he would just push the cart directly against the door to get it open, rather than making the effort to first push the door open with his hand. The daily ramming of the metal cart against the wooden door was causing the unsightly scratches.

It wasn't just laziness at the root of the problem. It was apathy. Whoever was putting the scratches on the door clearly did not care.

Because of class schedules and player availability, it was rarely the same player who pushed the cart back into the locker room every day. By the time I noticed what was happening, it was hard to pinpoint who was causing the scratches on the door. This made it a team problem.

I felt the locker room door was important because it was symbolic of the main entry point into our team, into our culture. What message were we sending by taking such poor care of it? Its appearance was not reflective of the pride we should have had for our team. In my mind, it was the equivalent to allowing the opening gates at Disney World to be scratched and tarnished, thereby putting into question the quality of what lay behind those gates. No Disney cast member would ever allow that to happen. Why should our team allow it to happen with our door?

I addressed the door issue with the team, but the significance of the scratches wasn't translating. They saw it as me nitpicking and as having little relevance to their needs. As far as they were concerned, the door was still functional, and the scratches weren't that big of a deal. I saw it as a microcosm of a much bigger problem—a lack of pride. Not enough of them cared.

The next chance I got, I gathered the entire team together in the hallway in front of the locker room door. I reiterated my feelings on the door being a symbolic gateway to our team. Then, I pulled out two uniforms. The first was our brand new uniform, which all of the players loved. The other was a faded, sweat-stained uniform from several years back. I asked the players which uniform they would prefer to wear. They unanimously pointed at the new uniform. I asked them why.

They gave answers like, "Because we look good in them," and "Because they feel good when you put them on." They were the kind of replies that you would expect.

Then, I asked them why they wouldn't want to wear the old uniform? Their answers solidified my point. They responded with: "Because people would think we're bums." "Nobody would take us seriously." "The other team would say we didn't have any self-respect."

I knew by their answers that they had pride and that they understood pride, but they weren't embracing the same level of pride in the locker room door as they were in their uniforms. I told them the stories about Disney. I made sure to stress the importance of paying attention to details, and that when you care about something, everything under that heading matters.

I genuinely believed the message was received this time. However, I was not convinced the team comprehended what it would take to repair the scratched door or the unnecessary inconvenience it would cause for someone to have to do the job.

As they all stood there staring at the scratches, I handed the team captain the tools and stain it was going to take to restore the door. I then had the entire team stay there until they finished the job. I wanted them to have an appreciation for the time and effort it took, and I wanted them to take pride in the work they all did. I asked them to all remain until the job was complete, so they were all involved in the process.

I didn't care about the quality of their work, to be honest. The idea was for them to understand the need to care about all aspects of the team, to take pride in the locker room door, and all of our other team identifiers going forward.

There are two reasons why a good teammate needs to care. The first is because it nullifies the need for disruptive leadership styles like micromanagement. It allows players to have a quiet mind and coaches to concentrate on teaching and building, as opposed to enforcing and punishing. The motives of players who care are easy to grasp. Likewise, a player who cares is coachable and can be assigned a role within the organization, even if it is not the most glamorous or sought-after position. The player will understand that every role is crucial to the team's overall success.

This hits on the great paradox of being a good teammate. Teammates who care must also *not* care about who gets the credit. They must have an ego, but it must be a team ego and not an individual ego.

The second reason a good teammate needs to care is because it promotes harmony between teammates. It gives them shared values and commonality, which eliminates pettiness and unresolvable internal conflicts. Players need to care about each other.

The first component is about *leader-to-follower* tranquility, whereas the second is about *peer-to-peer* tranquility. It encourages a sense of community and emotionally links teammates to one another. Bonds are formed that strengthen the players' commitment to the team. It also generates empathy, which, I continue to emphasize, always leads to trust and thinking about how your actions affect the other members of the team.

When I was a kid, and on the rare occasion when our home had running water, we had to be conscious of everyone else living in the house. The water pressure was low, and if you flushed a toilet when somebody was in the shower, that person would get scalded. If you took too long in the shower, there wouldn't be enough hot water left for the next person. You had to be constantly considerate of the other members of the family and think of the ramifications before you acted.

Teammates who care will do this. They comprehend how the actions of every member of the team interrelate. There is a ripple effect to every choice a teammate makes. As a coach, it is imperative that you have structures in place to prevent the ripple effect from causing divisions within the team.

Anytime a collection of individuals with varying backgrounds is brought together to form a team, there is the probability that team members will seek to identify the differences between themselves and their teammates. There is an innate human desire to be unique. Strong bonds are formed through commonality, not through differences.

Every team I have ever been associated with had diversity. Sometimes the basis was race and ethnicity. Sometimes the basis was geography. Sometimes the basis was social and economic differences. The nature of sports causes this to be the case for nearly every team. With all of these different backgrounds coming together, how do you get teammates to see their similarities as more prominent than their more obvious differences?

With college basketball players, I have to get them to see that, despite their varying backgrounds, every one of them has defied the odds to be where they are today. The often-cited NCAA statistics for the long-shot probability of a high school athlete becoming a college athlete do not account for any racial, geographical, or socio-economic origins. They simply outline how unlikely it is for any high school athlete to make it to the college level. The ability to defy the odds is what every one of my team members has in common. It is my responsibility to get them to see this similarity as greater than any difference they may identify.

In doing so, I must be sure not to allow them to discount completely their uniqueness, as diversity can be a legitimate asset to a team. Complete conformity can lead to stagnation, and it can threaten the potential growth of a team. All I am aiming to do is get them to realize that their similarities are more important than their differences.

Very often we hear stories in the media about a financially disadvantaged player who struggled in his early years, only to have his participation in sports reward him with wealth and fame. Those rags-to-riches stories are always inspiring, but maybe the player's success is not so much because of their participation in sports, as it is because of their work ethic and determination.

In reality, it may take more courage and determination for a kid who comes from sound financial means to make it as a college athlete than it does for the financially disadvantaged kid.

How many other choices did the poor kid have? How many other recreational options were there to compete with his participation in sports? Working hard to earn a spot on a college roster may have been the most logical and viable option he had. Sports were woven into the fabric of his life because they were his salvation.

For the financially secure, however, sports were a sacrifice because there were a lot of other options. Their families had the means to afford numerous alternative recreational and extracurricular activities—musical lessons, video games, amusement parks, etc. Those kids had to sacrifice involvement in all of those alternatives in their pursuit to play college sports. That takes focus and will-power, not to mention courage. How hard was it for them to turn down those other activities, many of which were seen as more reasonable and convenient options? Kids from financially secure families had to put in just as much training time and effort to make it as a college athlete as the poor kids, and their resolve to do so is indeed something they both have in common with everybody on the team.

The point is that if a coach is going to champion the cause of accentuating the importance of learning to be a good teammate, then he must get players to draw on their connection and commonality over their individuality and dissimilarities.

I'll end this chapter by re-visiting the Lou Holtz quote from the opening paragraph of this chapter about anything being solvable if enough people care. The primary reason it is important to teach players to care is because when they get into the real world and realize they are part of other teams, perhaps enough of them will care enough to solve society's most plaguing problems.

7

AN ORANGEMAN FROM VERMONT— THE FOURTH FACE ON MY MOUNT RUSHMORE

I HAVE been blessed to have crossed paths with a few really good coaches during my life. For example, when I left Garrett College, I went to play for Gary Nottingham at the University of South Carolina-Upstate. He had a brilliant basketball mind, although I am not always sure I understood just how brilliant he was at the time.

Several years later, after I had already embarked on my coaching career, he had left South Carolina and was working as an assistant coach for Bruce Weber at the University of Illinois. I had some opportunities to attend their practices and games and watch Nottingham from a much different perspective.

On one occasion, during Illinois' magical 2004–05 season with Deron Williams, Luther Head, and Dee Brown—a year in which the Illini went 29–0 to start the season and eventually advanced to the NCAA National Championship game—I was watching the team's practice and appreciated how talented Nottingham was. It occurred to me how I derived many of my on-court philosophies from things I had learned during the relatively short amount of time I played for him. Nottingham was a master of seeing things develop on the court.

While I respected the tactical side of his coaching and came to genuinely like him as a person, I never really had the same kind of connection with him that I had with Burt or Gibson. It wasn't until I became a college coach that I came across another mentor with whom I connected with on a level comparable to those two.

Tim Kelly—the fourth face on my Mount Rushmore—was the athletic director from whom I received my first college head coaching job. I had never seen any superior, be it a coach or a boss, who spoke as respectfully to his subordinates as Kelly did. He was a big man, and his physique could have easily been intimidating, but he personified Teddy Roosevelt's motto, "Speak softly and carry a big stick."

Kelly possessed the same capacity to care and share as Burt and Gibson, but he brought something else to the table, too. He had a special gift when it came to dealing with people. Working under him was a considerably different experience than I had previously had with persons of authority. His willingness to listen to his subordinates accounted for a large portion of the third part of my definition of a good teammate—good teammates listen.

Like the other men on my Mount Rushmore, Kelly was a product of his life experiences, and those experiences shaped his leadership philosophies. His basketball coaching background didn't follow the typical model, and much like Burt and Gibson, that scenario played a role in how he interacted with players.

Originally from the Syracuse, New York area, he grew up a devoted fan of Syracuse University athletic teams. He could recall with vivid clarity the details of seemingly every Syracuse victory. He knew the names and numbers of even the most obscure players. His memory and ability to regale willing listeners with these tales were astounding.

After graduating from Marcellus High School, he received a New York Regents Scholarship and enrolled at Cortland State. The duration of his time there, however, was short-lived. He discovered the party scene and his grades plummeted. In what he would later describe as his "academic debacle," Kelly attained an unenviable 0.00-grade point average. Cortland's administration promptly dismissed him at the end of his third semester.

Kelly spent the next few years working several manual labor jobs. He was a caretaker for a cemetery, a maintenance worker for the Onondaga County Highway Department, and a groundskeeper for his church parish. The last job, in what may be a prime example of things serendipitously working out the way they are supposed to, provided Kelly with his first real foray into coaching.

During the winter months, a groundskeeper in upstate New York did not have a lot of outdoor work, so Kelly was put in charge of running the church's hall, which contained a basketball court and two bowling alleys where bowlers still had to manually set their pins. The church hall served as an afterschool hangout for the community's youth, and Kelly started organizing and coaching Catholic Youth Organization (CYO) basketball teams for the kids. He liked strategizing and coaching the games and quickly developed an affinity for the craft.

Eventually, deciding it was time for a change, he and a friend moved north in search of jobs and a new chapter in their lives. They ended up in Vermont, working for a plastic manufacturer. The company's main product was airplane toilet seats. Kelly's job was to rough finish the seats and knock off the excess plastic whenever they came out of the mold. Although he didn't mind the work, he didn't see a future in it and he had concerns about the long-term effects the chemicals would have on his health.

While still working for the plastic company, Kelly started dating a girl who lived in the apartment below him. As it turned out, the girl's father owned one of Vermont's famous maple syrup companies. In time, the two married and her father offered Kelly a management-level position within the company. After several months of learning the business, he became the production manager at American Maple Products in Newport, Vermont.

He enjoyed the maple syrup business and his new position, but somehow he couldn't quite shake the coaching bug and began to volunteer his services in the local junior basketball programs. The varsity basketball coach at North Country Union High School took notice and asked Kelly to consider coaching his junior varsity team. That coach would turn out to be Gerry Clifford, the legendary Vermont high school coach and father of Steve Clifford—the coach Michael Jordan hired in 2013 to lead the Charlotte Bobcats NBA franchise.

Kelly was later promoted to be the elder Clifford's top varsity assistant, but the schedule he kept was challenging for Kelly and his now growing family.

He would go to work at the maple syrup factory at 5:00 in the morning, work all day, and then drive to coach basketball at North Country. When practice ended, he would return to work at the factory until around 10:00 at night. Somewhere along the way, his father-in-law decided to retire and split control of the company. Kelly assumed control over the operational side of the business while his brother-in-law took the reins of the financial side.

The continued long days away from his family and divided loyalties caused Kelly's wife to pose a very frank question to her husband: "What do you want to do with your life?" When he expressed a desire to coach, a plan was put in place where he would sell his half of the maple syrup business to his brother-in-law and go back to college to become a certified teacher.

That fall, Kelly enrolled at Lyndon State College and began classes to finish his degree. During his second year there, an unexpected opportunity presented itself. As often was the case at smaller NAIA colleges at that time, coaches were forced to coach multiple sports. At Lyndon State, Skip Pound served as the athletic director, head baseball coach, and head basketball coach. That August, the college's soccer coach resigned just before the start of the season, and Pound would have to also coach the soccer team.

With his time now being occupied with additional coaching responsibilities, and Kelly conveniently available, Pound allowed Kelly to run the basketball team's preseason workouts. Kelly's first season with Lyndon State would ironically be NBA veteran Stan Van Gundy's last season as coach of Lyndon's rival Castleton State. Van Gundy left to become an assistant coach at Canisius College, and Pound eventually turned all of the men's basketball coaching responsibilities over to Kelly, based in part on a strong recommendation from Gerry Clifford.

Kelly would go on to lead Lyndon State to considerable success during his head coaching tenure, receiving Mayflower Conference Coach of the Year honors on two different occasions. The time he spent managing the maple syrup company served him well as a coach. He had a knack for forming meaningful relationships for those under his command and earning their trust.

When he worked at American Maple, he couldn't simply shout orders and get employees to do what he wanted just because he was in charge. With Vermont's low unemployment rate, Kelly had little leverage over his workers. If they did not like the way they were treated, they would just leave and get another job. Unnecessary employee turnover would wreak havoc on production and seriously jeopardize the business.

I suspect this taught him to communicate with his subordinates on a different level, and that skill carried over into his coaching interactions with his players, and eventually into his athletic director interactions with his coaches. I never felt like I worked *for* him, but rather *with* him. His players most certainly felt the same way.

There is a subtle, yet significant, difference between building trust and earning trust. A person builds trust through repeated actions over time. Even in Gibson's case, where time was limited, he still built trust with players through his recurrent deeds. Sometimes this took place in the form of reputation passed down through stories from one generation of Garrett players to the next.

It is possible, though, to earn trust through a single act. It can be an instantaneous occurrence, accomplished through something as simple as how the person responds to a sensitive issue.

Kelly was especially gifted at getting a person to arrive at the right conclusion without having to directly tell that person what to do. He once had a despondent Lyndon State player come to his office, ready to quit the team. It was how Kelly responded to the problem that earned his trust.

The player told Kelly that he wasn't coming back to school after the Thanksgiving break because he was worried about losing his longtime girlfriend, who was attending Vermont Tech. The expected response would be to tell the young, love-struck player how stupid of an idea that was and that he should grow up because he was acting immature. Use the classic "other fish in the sea" analogy, and then send him on his way. That reply, however, would have undoubtedly caused resentment and eroded his trust.

Instead, Kelly calmly listened to the player before asking him the questions that the player had clearly failed to ask himself. "What about your major? Vermont Tech doesn't have that major. Do you think you'll lose many credits if you transfer? Do you still have your car? Vermont Tech is only seventy miles away; do you think it would help if maybe you drove down there to see her more frequently? You have been dating since eighth grade, do you think perhaps the way you are feeling is just a natural reaction to being away from each other for the first time?"

He never tried to solve or answer players' problems. He attempted instead to lead them to the solution. With my limited coaching experience, I was bound to make novice mistakes when I first started working for Kelly, and whenever I did, he did the same thing to me in his role as athletic director.

If there was a problem and he wanted corrective action, he wouldn't bark out the command. He posed the desired action in the form of a question, which usually started with the words, "Do you think…" He then listened to the response. If the person didn't arrive at the conclusion he wanted, he would pose another question. By doing it that way, he never made the person feel like he didn't trust him or her to make the right decision.

His approach made the person feel like a trusted colleague whose opinion he sought and who had the opportunity to help the leader solve a problem. As I later learned from Sister Eric Marie, helping others is something people inherently want to do, and it makes them feel better about themselves.

It takes a certain amount of self-confidence to be able to lead this way. An insecure coach may be less inclined to risk being perceived as anything but authoritarian. But the funny thing is, Kelly had earned so much trust that his authority was the strongest of all. Subordinates wanted to please him, and they were exceptionally loyal to him. When the proverbial *it* hit the fan, subordinates were there to support him.

Along those lines, Kelly also earned trust because he knew the first thing to do when it did hit the fan—turn off the fan.

One time we had a fundraiser to purchase new workout equipment and the students had set out a jar on the front desk of the Health and Fitness Center for donations. Students and community members who used the facility would drop loose change in the jar from time to time. We had one student-athlete, though, who started helping himself to the jar's contents. At first, under the guise of getting change for the vending machines, he would drop a dollar in the jar but take out more than the equivalent amount of coins.

After a while, it got to the point where he was blatantly taking change out of the jar for the vending machines and not even bothering to put bills in first. Others started to notice what this student, who happened to be very popular and well liked, was doing and they brought it to Kelly's attention.

The first thing Kelly did was remove the jar from the front desk. He didn't yell and scream and berate the student. He didn't get defensive about whose fault it was and try to deflect blame, or for that matter, even attempt to assign blame. He was focused on ending the problem. By concentrating on the solution and not the offender, he earned the trust of everyone watching. In essence, he turned off the fan.

Kelly left Lyndon State to become the athletic director at Mount Aloysius College in Pennsylvania. The school was in a state of flux when he arrived. Its enrollment had plummeted in recent years, and its financial state was far from healthy. An outside consulting firm had been brought in to examine the situation. One of the firm's recommendations was for the college to make the transition from the NAIA to the NCAA and boost its enrollment through growth in its athletic programs. They charged Kelly with this task.

Coaches come in all shapes and sizes, and I have heard a lot of stories over the years of how various coaches got their first jobs. But I have heard few that rival the story of how I came to be employed as the basketball coach at Mount Aloysius.

My predecessor, whom Kelly had hired, was in his third season at Mount Aloysius when they terminated him. He had previously been an NCAA Division I assistant at several colleges and was certainly qualified for the job, but there had been a few anger management episodes leading up to the event that ultimately broke the camel's back and resulted in his dismissal.

Scheduling games was not an easily accomplished task during the college's period of transition. For those reasons, the coach had arranged an exhibition game to be played at a nearby prison against the inmates' team. Make no mistake about it, those prison teams can have some very talented players on them. Unfortunately, more than a few high-level Division I and professional athletes who made poor life choices found themselves behind bars, playing for the prison team. At some point during the game, the coach went off on the referees for what he believed to be poor officiating. His actions allegedly sent the gymnasium into chaos and nearly started a prison riot. Coaches were restrained and players were rushed out of the facility for their safety.

Kelly was greeted by phone calls the next morning from the prison director and the game's officials. The coach was relieved of his duties soon after this incident. Some of the players later told me the ordeal was one of the most intense and frightening moments they had ever experienced.

I was working as a local high school coach and was named as his replacement a few days later. It was simply a matter of me being in the right place at the right time and the job offered under circumstances that alienated more experienced candidates.

Mount Aloysius was a challenging situation, but working for Kelly was not. Some of my best coaching memories are of the two of us sitting down for lunch at local restaurants and talking basketball. We would use the salt and pepper shakers to script out plays and discuss game strategy. He was insightful and very generous in sharing his knowledge. But more so, he always listened to my ideas, no matter how outlandish they may have been.

Kelly never gave the impression that he had an ulterior motive, nor gave anyone reason not to trust him. He came across as very humble, and reinforced that by his appearance and actions.

He was not a flashy dresser, no expensive shoes or anything like that. The only jewelry I ever recall him wearing was his wedding band and a very plain wristwatch. When you looked at him, there was nothing that suggested vanity. The simplicity of his appearance put people at ease and encouraged immediate trust. It was clear he was not going to be self-absorbed with his private agenda. He looked like someone who was trustworthy.

Imagine a scenario where you are hanging off of a cliff, help-lessly holding on for dear life. Out of nowhere, three outstretched arms appear, each ready to rescue you.

When you look up, you notice one of the arms belongs to a man wearing a Rolex and an expensive Armani suit. He has per-fectly shined leather shoes and a slicked back hairstyle that is right out of the pages of *Gentleman's Quarterly*.

Tattoos cover the next arm. The person is garbed in Goth attire, complete with black lipstick and piercings in places you didn't even know it was possible to pierce.

The third arm is quite ordinary. The man is dressed very plain. He appears clean and neatly groomed. There is nothing particularly noteworthy about his appearance.

Which one do you choose to trust under those circumstances? Questions will rush through your mind. If you pick the first arm, will he let you go if you accidentally scratch his Rolex? What will happen if he scuffs his shoe or if the seams on his suit start to tear? Why is he even willing to help you? What does he have to gain?

How about the second arm? Is he offering it to you so he can drop you for his pleasure and watch you fall in some twisted, sadis-tic act? With all of those piercings, is this person capable of making sound decisions?

I've come to learn that there is truth to the idea that you can-not judge a book by its cover. Any of those three persons could be trustworthy and offering a legitimate helping hand. But in that instant, whose appearance earned your immediate trust—or at least gave you the fewest reasons not to trust? In reality, people make initial judgments quite frequently based on appearance. How a person dresses affects your perception. You can earn trust by something as simple as how you dress.

Like some of the other men I have written about, Kelly was also able to set his ego aside. He was willing to do those jobs that others might have perceived as being beneath them. This attitude wasn't limited to only jobs, either.

No person was ever beneath him. Kelly was very bright and well read, but he could relate to people from all walks of life—most likely another byproduct of his time working at the maple syrup company. He had to interact with blue-collar factory workers, salesmen, and a variety of other corporate personalities. This experience rendered him capable of being comfortable with all types of people. He could, and would, speak with professors and maintenance workers on equal terms.

Kelly's general method of operation was to treat everybody the same, *differently*. It was a concept that he had learned and implemented long ago. He applied it to how he treated his players as a coach and continued to make use of it as an administrator. His ability to do this contributed significantly to his earning the trust of others.

One time, I was having an issue with a particular member of the maintenance staff. I had just come back from a recruiting trip and was returning the college's fleet car that I had used to its designated parking lot, which was located beside the physical plant office.

At Mount Aloysius, the maintenance department was in charge of the fleet cars. When I stepped out of the car, one of the older, more cantankerous maintenance guys started to give me grief about bringing the car back so dirty and wanted to know why I didn't have the decency to wash it before I returned it.

I had just driven several hours through a snowstorm for a less than fruitful recruiting excursion, and I was, as they say, strung out from the road. The guy caught me off guard with his confrontation, and I didn't know what to say, nor how to take him. His comments irritated me and got under my skin.

The car was filthy. I couldn't deny that fact. The all-too-familiar salt residue that accompanies our Pennsylvania winters covered the car. My initial reaction was to point out to him in colorfully clear language that it wasn't my job to clean the cars. It was his. And if he didn't like it, he was welcome to kiss my readily available derriere. I instead chose to wisely ignore him and say nothing. At any rate, I thought it was wise at the time.

When I walked back into the office after the encounter, I was very annoyed. My anger was festering. Kelly could sense something was bothering me and asked what happened. After I gave him the details, he chuckled and made a comment along the lines of me needing to use some humor with the situation. His response only further annoyed me. I thought it was some slight on me for taking the situation too seriously—which in hindsight I probably was. Fortunately, I had enough patience left to reply with a non-confrontational, "What do you mean?"

In typical Kelly-esque fashion, he clarified his response. "Do you think it would work out better, if the next time that happens, you asked him what our poor criminal students would have to do if you washed the car?" He wanted me to use humor with the guy, as opposed to anger.

At Mount Aloysius, wayward students—those who find themselves having broken one of the college's rules, such as violating the underage alcohol policy—are often penalized with on-campus community service hours. They are usually put at the disposal of the maintenance department who commonly gave them the task of cleaning the fleet cars. The maintenance guys loved it when the student workers were assigned to them, mainly because it got them out of doing some of the menial tasks that they did not enjoy.

Several weeks later, I returned from another recruiting trip and had the same type of confrontation with the same cantankerous maintenance worker. Only this time, I took Kelly's advice and responded with the whimsical comment about our criminal students having nothing to do if I cleaned the cars. It was silly—but it worked!

The maintenance guy laughed hard, and we became friends after that. As strange as it sounds, I always felt I earned his trust in that exact moment. He no longer seemed insulted. He didn't believe I thought his work as beneath me.

I avoided an unnecessary confrontation by appealing instead to his sense of humor, a more desired emotion for anyone. When a person is put in a position where he has to fight, he will instinctively be leery of the motives of the other person. If another emotion replaces anger, like humor or happiness, trust can be earned.

Kelly was good at using his humor skills to navigate the complicated and political side of academia. I found it to be exasperating, if not demoralizing. He was able to focus on the issue and not the people involved. He was good at suppressing the frustrations of those working under him when it came to dealing with bureaucratic red tape.

One of the ways he did this was by laying out roles and expectations in advance. He told me he also used to do this for his players whenever he coached. If a player was going to be the team's backup big man, he would talk to him at the beginning of the season and tell him exactly how many minutes he expected him to get every game, and when he thought those minutes would occur. He also conveyed to the player what he specifically expected from him when he was on the court. For instance, he might say something like, "You're only going to play four minutes. I don't care if you get in foul trouble, so I expect you to use your fouls before you allow their player to score a lay-up."

Some leaders may worry that this approach could lead to a player plateauing. They like the more traditional idea of pitting players against each other and having them compete for playing time. Perhaps it could lead to each player contributing more, but it could also be bad for the team. This type of competition has the potential to undermine selflessness and lead to cliques and players building silos. It doesn't lead to the production of good teammates.

Players were happy because Kelly explained their role. They may not have always liked their role, but they disliked, even more, the feeling of uncertainty about where they fit in. Kelly's way earned their trust because he satisfied their need to belong and understand where they fit into the team.

The other thing Kelly did to suppress the angst of his subordinates was to keep them in the loop. Not only was I the head men's basketball coach, but I was also an assistant athletic director. Any time he came back from an administrative meeting, he immediately informed me of what was going on. He didn't have to disclose every detail, but he always relayed the important bullet points.

Many times it was as basic as, "This is what we have to do. This why we have to do it. And, this is when we have to do it." I never felt he was secretive with information, and he never let it seem like he was hiding sensitive material from me. The openness of his communication led to earned trust.

If I had later found out that he had kept something secret from me, I would have questioned his intentions. If this happened, what possible conclusion could I draw except that he did not trust me? Even if he countered with, "Well, I was instructed not to tell anybody else," it would still call into question his level of trust in me, and it would have built feelings of resentment and broken the relationship.

In a roundabout way, Kelly was continually grooming me to be his replacement, whether or not that was something I aspired to be. I didn't particularly want to be an athletic administrator, but I don't know if that mattered to him. It was just how he operated. He would have done the same thing no matter who was sitting in my position.

He created an atmosphere that from the moment an employee started their job, they had an obligation to train their eventual replacement, and he viewed himself as no exception. This created continuity, and moreover, it earned trust. Good teammates engage in this practice because it demonstrates a commitment to something bigger than themselves.

Kelly never guarded his knowledge. He freely shared what he had learned with me and was always approachable. Because he was open and willing to train me, I didn't sense that I was ever set up to fail or that he was protective of his position. This arrangement did not threaten him, but allowed him to listen because he was not concerned with protecting his authority.

I also appreciated Kelly's perspective on coaches and teams. He didn't obsess over records or margin of victory. He looked at teams as a process—from where they started to where they finished. He felt a good coach was able to move the team forward through that process. That was a good thing for me, especially in the early going, because my teams didn't win many games when I started at Mount Aloysius. My very first team went 0-12 before we finally won our first game. Kelly's support never wavered during that time.

In my estimation, Kelly is a wonderful example of how even the leader of an organization has the capacity and responsibility to be a good teammate. The head of the household, the CEO of a corporation, the pastor of the church, or anyone in a position of leadership should embody the notion that a good teammate cares, shares, and listens. Their rank should not excuse them from doing those things.

8

GOOD TEAMMATES LISTEN

I HAVE heard it said that we have two ears and one mouth for a reason—because we are supposed to listen twice as much as we speak. If caring is the most desirable quality of a good teammate, then listening is the most uncommon.

In the late 17th century, a British businessman named John Castaing began posting a list of stock and commodity prices on the wall of a coffee house in London. Although merchants around the world had been trading goods for generations, Castaing's posting of that list is considered the origin of the stock market as we now know it.[39]

Today, gold, silver, crude oil, and other valuable commodities are traded on stock exchange floors in London, Tokyo, Shanghai, and New York. The trade market floors decide the fate of the global economy. You could make a case that even more valuable commodities are doled out via an entirely different market—the black market. Illegal drugs, stolen passports, and counterfeit cigarettes account for big money in the underground economy.

I would argue, however, that nothing bought and sold on either of those markets represents our most valuable commodity. Walk into the oncology wing of any hospital in the world and you quickly realize that the most valuable commodity is time. It can't be mined, grown, or reproduced in any capacity. When it's gone, it's gone. Every living being values time and only has a limited supply.

Listening is a prized component of a good teammate because listening is a reflection of the value you place on another's time. You listen because you respect the speaker's time. What could go further in earning trust than how you demonstrate respect for a person's most valued possession?

The act of listening is uncommon because it's not easy to do. It doesn't come naturally. It takes a concentrated effort. Most people are born with the ability to hear, but not necessarily the ability to listen. In my experience, players fall into three different categories of listeners, which I liken to three different types of sponges.

The first type of player is comparable to an old, dry sponge. Its texture is so hardened that it no longer absorb waters, no matter how much you pour on it. This listener is so concerned with thinking about what he is going to say next that the speaker's message goes unabsorbed, deflected from his mind as the water rolling off the old, rigid sponge. Ironically, this "sponge" is in actuality often too self-absorbed to care about anything other than his own words.

The second type is like a low-quality sponge purchased from a discount store. It is useable but not as absorbent as you would ideally like it to be. Under duress, it usually falls apart. This type of listener hears what the speaker is saying, but is unable to extract meaning from the message. He might be able to repeat your words with accuracy, but if you ask him to explain what you meant, he wouldn't know.

My wife once mentioned, tongue in cheek, that she was going to write a book one day titled, *Funny Things Players Have Said to My Husband*. Some of my favorite entries into this yet-to-materialize work of literature are good examples of the second type of listener.

For instance, I had one of my all-time favorite players pose a puzzling question to me during his freshman year. Though possessing an unusual physique—he was only six-feet-two-inches tall, but wore a size-18 shoe and resembled the letter "L" when turned sideways—he was extremely well liked. He had a gentle innocence about him.

This was around the time that Nolan Richardson, the legendary coach from the University of Arkansas, had things rolling with the Razorbacks basketball team. He had been using the phrase "Forty minutes of Hell" to describe the intensity with which his team played and the experience they gave their opponents. Forty minutes was the length of an entire college basketball game, meaning his team never let up on its pressure. I was trying to copy this intensity and had dubbed the portion of our practice where we were going to work on our defensive intensity as "Forty minutes of Hell."

With genuine curiosity, the player with the oversized feet asked me, "How long is forty minutes of Hell?" (In a less formal setting, I would probably insert an obligatory "lol" or "smh" at this point.)

Another time, we were dividing up teams for a drill, and I asked a player to pick a number between one and five. With complete sincerity, he responded, "Six."

We are sometimes so subconsciously programmed to answer an anticipated question that we reply without listening to the question. In this case, I suspect that player was expecting me to have him pick a number between the usual one and ten.

Have you ever had the experience of bumping into someone who offered a casual, "What's going on?" only for you to reply, "Pretty good" because you thought they were going to ask, "How are you?" It happens to everybody. The odd thing is when the person who asked the original question continues talking without noticing your response. It is a double example of messages not registering.

The last type of listener is the high-quality, ultra-absorbent sponge that is as good as they come. It soaks up everything and dispenses what it absorbed. This is the model player. He not only hears the message, but takes it in, processes it, and then applies it exactly the way it was intended. This is the way a good teammate listens.

Those who employ this third kind of listening reveal their level of engagement with supportive body language. They understand that body language is as important a form of communication as actual verbal communication. A telltale sign of a person who's listening on this level is that he or she affirmatively nods his or her head as the speaker is talking.

Dick DeVenzio, the founder of the world-renowned Point Guard College, mentions this idea in his wonderfully written book *Stuff Good Players Should Know*. Tim Kelly introduced me to DeVenzio and his book when I started working for him at Mount Aloysius. Although DeVenzio wrote the book over 30 years ago, its value still resonates. I often tell the parents of aspiring basketball players who attend my camp that if they want to give their child an edge, they should buy their child this book. It is filled with nuggets of wisdom that can legitimately impact a player's game.

On the topic of listening and nodding, DeVenzio says that when the player nods his head, he gives the coach extra satisfaction, and that can keep the coach energized to continue helping the player.[40] The listener isn't nodding his head for himself as much as he is for the speaker.

Naturally, listeners can process messages without nodding their heads, but this simple act further substantiates the concept of being a good teammate. The nodding of the head communicates feedback to the speaker. It shows that he is willing to share in the conversation. It shows he is paying attention and cares about the message delivered. It shows he is a receptive listener.

There is certainly duality to a good teammate listening. The subordinate must listen to the instructions of the superior; therefore, a player must listen to the instructions of his coach. A teammate must also listen to his peers so he can hear relayed instructions. Listening also helps him learn what his teammates are feeling and thinking. Listening allows him to empathize with his teammates.

When I wrote the children's book *Be a Good Teammate*, I made sure to include both of those ideas. But when it came time to illustrate them, I struggled. The page that read, "I listen to my coach" was relatively easy do. I just drew a coach with his arm around a player's shoulder, offering instruction to the youngster.

The page that read "I also listen to my teammates" was more challenging. I wasn't sure how exactly to capture it. I thought about drawing a picture with kids on the court discussing strategy and technique. I was fearful, though, that people might misunderstand

and think that talking was the significant action or that the listeners were subordinate. This is not what I wanted to convey. I wanted people to view all of the players with equal standing.

I thought about having one player standing up and addressing the team while all of his teammates gathered around him, but that contained the same problem in inequality. The act of listening wasn't intended to be about leadership or players taking charge, which I felt this picture would suggest. It was supposed to be more about peer-to-peer listening where you listen because you respect the thoughts and opinions of your fellow teammates and vice versa.

I finally decided upon a drawing of three players having a conversation in a locker room. A girl player and a boy player are sitting down on opposite benches while another boy player is standing behind them holding a towel with one of his legs propped up on the bench. The way it was drawn, it is impossible to tell which player is the primary speaker. They appear as though any of them could be listening to what the other two are saying. There is no main speaker in the picture, and, therefore, no delegated listener.

Interestingly, when we first starting showing proof copies of the children's book to parents and teachers of its intended age group, someone pointed out that boys and girls were both in the locker room and wondered if that was an accurate portrayal. My response was that readers needed to suspend their perception of conventional methods and see the location as symbolic.

In the locker room, everybody is on equal terms. They might not be on the court, because of stats or playing time. But in the locker room, everybody is a member of the team, and only members of the team are allowed in the locker room. It is a special place for teams. Besides, who is to say that a co-ed youth team wouldn't meet at halftime in a designated location like a locker room?

Whenever players get out in the real world, they are going to enter an even more politically correct environment where they will have to be tolerant and respectful of the opinions of their co-workers. Teaching players to be good peer-to-peer listeners is setting them up to enter the workforce having already acquired this essential skill.

I find it unfortunate that our schools require classes that aim to improve communication skills like reading, writing, and speaking—but not listening. Before I started my career as a coach, I worked briefly as a morning show disc jockey on a radio station. My stretch in that profession was an education in effective communication, particularly effective listening. You might expect that working in radio mandates that you place a premium on speaking; but quite the contrary, listening was often the more critical skill.

In the course of normal conversation, you can lose your train of thought, but it isn't always a big deal when you get caught not listening to the person speaking. If you lose your train of thought on the air, you come across as an idiot. It can be very embarrassing. When you are sitting in the studio around the control board with the other members of the morning show, it can be even worse. The nature of the situation and the vibrant personalities in the morning radio business can humiliate you when this happens. The best chance to avoid this humiliation is to be focused and listen carefully.

On our show, we made an effort to keep our conversations concise. The program director didn't want any long monologs, or for any of us to commit the radio gaffe of "stepping on the toes" of the other disc jockeys, i.e. talking simultaneously. To prevent these, we had a system where we would speak in about six-second increments and then offer a quick pause. The pause didn't necessarily have to mark the end of the speaker's message, or be an indication for the others to start speaking. It was just an opportunity for the listeners to acknowledge they heard the speaker. Typically, this took the form of us interjecting a simple "okay" or "uh huh" before the speaker carried on.

To avoid simultaneous talking, we would hold up a finger to indicate to the others that we had something to say. It was an exaggerated version of students holding up their hands, waiting for the teacher to call on them. I also became acutely attuned to look for the identifiable facial expression that nearly all people make when they want to speak. There is a delicate popping of their lips, just before their mouths open ever so slightly. If someone has something to say but are politely resisting the urge to speak over the top of the person currently speaking, they start to make this face and then freeze. I looked for my coworkers doing this. I even noticed myself making the same expression whenever I had something to add and one of the others was already talking. In fact, it became incredibly frustrating to me when I did this in conversations with people outside of the radio show, and they didn't keep to the six-second rule or recognize me making *the* face.

On a semi-related note, I think one of the best things I got out of my radio days, besides the six-second rule, was a newfound appreciation for time. We waste so much time in the day because we routinely overestimate how long things take to do. In radio, there is always a countdown. This song will end in this many seconds. You have this long until the next commercial. Through experience, I learned that a tremendous amount of activity can happen within the confines of a two-minute commercial break.

In the building that housed our station, the closest restroom was at the end of a lengthy hallway, which meant you had to walk out of the studio, exit the glass doors of our suite, and then walk a hundred yards down the corridor to get to the restroom. Disc jockeys were supposed to take care of things before they went on the air, but if nature happened to call during your time on air, you always had a long song on standby for just this situation. Obviously, this was in the days before computer-hosted music databases and voice-tracked or cyber-jockeyed broadcasts. Songs were still manually loaded back then.

One early morning I was on-air by myself, and I felt nature calling. I loaded my designated "restroom song"—a near five-minute Aerosmith ballad—and headed down the hallway. The moment I heard the glass office doors click behind me, however, I realized there was a problem.

It was a national holiday, so the regular office staff wasn't around that day, nor were any of my fellow morning show disc jockeys. The doors locked behind me, and I had left my keys and cell phone inside the studio. Nobody was there to let me back in the studio when the song ended. Simultaneous talking may have been bad radio etiquette, but dead air was much worse.

If I learned anything from my time in England with Burt, it was the value of having a contingency plan. Burt always prepared for the unexpected, and I learned from him to do the same. In case I ever got locked out of the radio station, I had extra keys made and kept them in the glove box of my car. I remembered this and swiftly ran to my car, which I had parked in the lot at the other end of the building, to retrieve those extra keys.

Unfortunately, when I arrived at my car, it was also locked. However, I had prepared for this scenario too. In case I ever locked myself out of my car, I hid a spare key underneath. In the darkness of a dimly lit parking lot, I slid under my car and found the spare key. I opened the car door and got the extra station keys out of the glove box. I rushed into the station, unlocked the office suite doors, and arrived back in the studio as the final seconds of the song were playing. No one listening to their radio had any idea how much had just transpired or that I had averted a broadcast tragedy.

I never forgot this lesson on the advantage of having a contingency plan or how much you can accomplish in a short time. This knowledge has served me well.

Clearly, my foresight to have a contingency plan in place wouldn't have happened if I hadn't listened to the advice of my former coach. From the player's perspective, it is sometimes easier to see the value in listening to the coach and not just in the aftermath of a ridiculous situation like this.

Players are mostly aware of the need to listen to their coach. When everyone listens to the coach's directions, they can implement the game plan. Everyone is on the same page. The coach is not distracted and forced to correct misdirected players. This harmony keeps players involved and prioritizing the best interests of the team.

I am a firm believer that mistakes are a part of sports. Mistakes are learning opportunities. With few exceptions, single errors rarely beat you on the court or in life. But repeated mistakes can be devastating. A player who listens to the coach limits the potential to repeat mistakes, and that is one of the reasons why a player who listens to the coach is a good teammate.

Countless strategies can be used to get players to become better listeners. As coaches, there are times when we probably do a disservice to the players' development by how we punish them for not listening. If a player doesn't follow a coach's instructions, the typical response is to subject that player to immediate negative consequences, such as wind sprints, pushups, or a seat on the bench. The Marine Corps operates similarly. If a soldier doesn't listen to his commander's instructions, he is immediately asked to "drop and give me twenty."

The real world doesn't work like this. They don't make an employee do pushups in the business sector for small mistakes. The consequences in corporate America for these kinds of transgressions are more delayed. They wait until your next performance review or the next round of downsizing to punish you. The consequences in the real world are frequently the lack of receiving a positive reward than some form of punishment. The employee gets passed over for a promotion or misses out on a bonus. Coaches could better prepare players for life after sports by utilizing this alternative practice. It is worth making an effort to reward players for listening and not punishing them for not listening.

Another way to earn trust and get players to listen is to help limit their distractions—a chaotic environment, academic concerns, girlfriend issues, etc. Many of these are beyond the scope of the coach's control. Creating an environment conducive to learning, however, is something a coach can influence.

As an undergrad, I had an interesting communications class, and one day the professor used dodgeballs to demonstrate the two-way nature of communication. He explained that the ball represented the speaker's message, and then he proceeded to toss the ball back and forth with students in the class. He made the analogy that effective communication only exists if the message is received, much as the receiver catches the ball.

As he tossed the ball to another student, somebody knocked at the classroom's door. The professor turned his head to see who was there, right as the student threw the ball back at him. The ball smashed the poor professor right in the face and sent his glasses crashing to the ground. Without missing a beat, the professor turned to the class and said, "That is how distractions can keep messages from being received the way they were intended."

Tim Kelly had a subtle way of alerting people that he was about to toss a metaphoric ball in their direction, so they could prepare themselves to receive it safely. He would listen intently to what the person had to say, without interrupting. As soon as the right moment presented itself, he asked, "Do you want to know what I think?"

What was the person going to say to this? No? In the unlikely event that he did, then he was proving himself to be an unabsorbent sponge, and Kelly's message would have been a moot point anyhow. When the person said yes, they were receptive to listening to whatever it was Kelly was about to say.

By hearing the speaker out and waiting until he was done to request permission to offer a response, Kelly seized the person's most approachable moment. Too often, coaches want to jump in and try to solve the player's problem too quickly. They think their expediency is a sign of efficiency, but that's not always true. Many times, the player's current problem is part of a much larger issue. The coach may miss out on discovering the truth if he interrupts too soon and does not listen to all of what the player has to say.

Art Markman, the author of the book *Smart Thinking and Habits of Leadership*, in a blog entry he wrote for the online business magazine *Fast Company*, equated this to "curing a symptom, but not curing the disease."[41]

I've tried to explain why good teammates listen to their coach and why they listen to their fellow teammates, but I haven't addressed why coaches should listen to their players—a frequently overlooked, yet important element of team-listening dynamics.

Teammates should listen to their coach because it minimizes mistakes and maximizes productivity. Teammates should listen to their fellow teammates because it conveys respect and leads to comradery. When a team is close-knit, it tends to stick together when seas get choppy. The skill of peer-to-peer listening is so vital that I almost feel teammates should be afforded the same legal rights as married couples in regards to testifying against one another.

Spousal privilege precludes an individual from testifying against his or her spouse. It also protects the confidential content of communication between spouses. It ensures that both parties can communicate freely among themselves without the threat of outside repercussions. Coaches would be wise to encourage this from players. Teammates should be permitted to communicate on this level and to have this same kind of freedom.

While coaches and players may never be able to enjoy the degree of freedom as peer-to-peer communication, it is nevertheless important for coaches to listen to their players. As far as that goes, listening to players no longer means just listening to their spoken words or their body language. It now additionally includes "listening" to the players' social media posts. You can gain insight into how a player is feeling and thinking based on his posts on Twitter or Instagram. A coach has an obligation to decipher what their players post. Social media outlets are more than modern day diaries: they are a means for Millennials to express their thoughts and communicate with their world.

An effective coach subscribes to the notion that a good idea can come from anywhere, and that is why he values the opinions of his players—even the ones that sit on the bench and don't often get to play. Beyond the belief that a good idea can come from anywhere, an effective coach should listen to all of his players' verbal, physical, and written messages because it shows he cares and keeps hope alive for the players. They don't get discouraged. Players still believe they can help make a difference and impact the team by expressing their opinions. Players feel like their views matter.

Coaches who listen like this also model healthy future leadership behaviors for their players. When the player's career is over, and he must move on with his life's work, he may eventually find himself in a position of management. If he follows his former coach's example, and he has a willingness to listen to the concerns of those under his command, he will attain their loyalty and become a beloved leader. That sort of leader has the potential to bring about change and positively impact society.

The idea that good teams talk on the court and the field has received a lot of attention recently. In the sport of basketball, for example, talking on the court may translate into players communicating on defense. They are supposed to call out the opposing player they are guarding or the defensive position they are moving into on the court. In theory, talking gives a team an improved chance of being successful.

Maybe this is true. I can see where this idea is coming from, but I counter it with a quote from Mahatma Gandhi: "Only speak if it improves upon the silence." Calling out instructions on defense might improve upon the silence, but only if other players listen to them. Good teams may talk, but the best teams listen.

9

ENTER THE PENGUIN—
ED'S SISTER THE SISTER

HUMANS are born with an inherent need to be loved. The experiments of psychologists like John Bowby (*Attachment Theory*) and many others have consistently confirmed this belief.[42] Part of being loved is being heard. Or perhaps more appropriately phrased for the theme of this book, being listened to.

Most people have had at least one person in their life that sincerely listened to their most intimate thoughts—their hopes, dreams, fears, and so forth—someone with a non-judgmental ear to whom they could vent about their problems. For me, that individual was my paternal grandmother, Lucille.

The grandchildren in our family called her "Gigi." Normally, it would be safe to assume the name originated from the underdeveloped speech mechanics of the first-born grandchild, but that wasn't the case. She chose the name because she felt she was too young to be called "grandma" or any other traditional derivative. She believed "Gigi" sounded, well, cooler.

This spoke volumes about my grandmother's vibrant personality. Although she was married for almost half of a century, she spent the bulk of her retired years as an independent, self-sufficient widow. My grandfather passed away at a relatively young age and she never remarried. Gigi lived well into her mid-90s, and that left a lot of time for her to wield her independence.

For whatever reasons, I have always been drawn to independent, strong-spirited, older women like my grandmother. When I was a student, some of my favorite teachers and professors were these types of females. I would go out of my way to gain their attention. I had a music teacher named Miss Smith whom I was especially fond of in middle school. She was spunky, and I adored her. Despite having no musical ability, nor the capacity or even the interest to sing, I joined the concert choir for the sole reason that Miss Smith was the instructor. She had a special way of connecting with kids, and I felt that connection as well as anybody. She retired the year after I graduated high school, and as a testament to her vivacious spirit, she went back to college to earn a doctorate degree.

After my grandmother had passed, there was a void in my life, and Sister Eric Marie emerged at the right time to fill that void. More than that, she became the person I saw as personifying the quintessential *good* teammate because she embodied all three of the defining characteristics: caring, sharing, and listening. For me, she was the person who put it all together.

When Sister Eric Marie walks into a room, you feel the mood of the room immediately lighten. You feel compelled to smile. Optimism floods your senses, and any pent-up stress you've been harboring seems to float magically away.

In Gretchen Rubin's bestselling book, *The Happiness Project: Or, Why I Spent a Year Trying to Sing in the Morning, Clean My Closets, Fight Right, Read Aristotle, and Generally Have More Fun*, she recounts the details of how she attempted to become a happier person. The book is an intriguing look at how much happier we can make ourselves with very minimal effort. Rubin mentions how contact with others can boost a person's mood.[43] This is a psychological phenomenon known as "emotional contagion" where both good and bad moods are unconsciously passed to others.[44]

In a research project for the Yale School of Management, Dr. Sigal Barsade conducted a study on the ripple effect of emotional contagion. In the study, Barsade had groups of business school students role-play a scenario where one member of the group pretended to be a department head lobbying for an employee to get a merit-based raise. The other members of the group acted as a salary committee charged with appropriately allocating the company's limited funds. Unbeknownst to the other members of the group, Barsdade assigned an actor to each group whose goal was to express one of four different moods—cheerful enthusiasm, serene warmth, hostile irritability, and depressed sluggishness—during the negotiation process.

The results of the study showed what a profound effect emotional contagion can have on group dynamics. Groups where the actor was able to convey positive emotion elevated the mood of the entire group. An increase in cooperation and a decrease in interpersonal conflict was additionally found to exist.[45] Sister Eric Marie's cheerful demeanor has this exact same effect on groups, which is what should happen when a good teammate joins the group.

I used to half-mockingly call the nuns around Mount Aloysius "penguins." Although they still dress very modestly, the Sisters of Mercy long ago abandoned the traditional black and white habit associated with the image of a nun. At first, the term was a tip of the hat to the famous scene in the movie *The Blues Brothers* where Jake and Elwood go back to visit their childhood orphanage. In the scene, Dan Aykroyd's character refers to the nun who runs St. Helen of the Blessed Shroud Orphanage as *the penguin*.[46] As I grew closer to Sister Eric Marie, the term came to be more a term of endearment.

Sister Eric Marie has always been a fan of the Mount Aloysius College basketball team. She comes to all of the games and cheers right along with our most passionate supporters. She has been a devotee of the men's basketball team from its inception. It is sometimes funny to me whenever we hold alumni events because every men's basketball player who comes back to visit has a story about Sister Eric Marie and inevitably greets her with a big hug.

She wasn't around very much, though, when I was first hired at Mount Aloysius. Her mother was ill at the time, and she had moved into her mother's home to take care of her on a nearly full-time basis. I rarely saw Sister Eric Marie during the beginning of my tenure, and what interactions I did have were very limited. I will, however, never forget one of my earliest encounters with her.

During my first few seasons of coaching, I had convinced myself that we were going to generate interest in the program and make a name for ourselves by playing extremely up-tempo basketball, like the Paul Westhead-led teams at Loyola Marymount. We became a high-flying, run-and-gun act. The players bought into the generous shot selection policy of taking the first shot they could get off. The problem was, although we were good shooters, we weren't good makers, and that led to us missing a lot of shots and losing a lot of games.

After a particularly bad loss, I walked out of the locker room and saw a couple of nuns still congregating in the gym. I made the mistake of walking over to them thinking they could provide me with some much-needed encouragement, and maybe convince them to offer up a few prayers for our struggling team. I did not get the response I had anticipated. One of them said to me, "Coach, God created all men equal, not all shooters." What she meant was, "Stop letting everybody on the team shoot the ball, and do a better job of setting up the good shooters."

Sister Eric Marie claims she wasn't the nun who said it. I didn't really know her that well at the time, and conceivably my memory could be cloudy, but nonetheless, I never forgot the advice.

Sister Eric Marie's brother, Ed "Buddy" Setlock, was a popular high school football coach and athletic director in his hometown. His health, unfortunately, was deteriorating from a battle with diabetes. After Sister Eric Marie's mother had passed, she remained at home to take care of her ailing brother until he also passed away. Although I never had the privilege of knowing Buddy personally, I did get a sense of how popular he was the only time I did get to meet him—at his wake.

I went to the funeral home to show my support for Sister Eric Marie because I understood how close she had been with her brother. As I pulled into the parking lot, I did not expect to see a line of people waiting to pay their respects winding around the front of the building. Her brother was described as a champion of the underdog, and the length of that line was an indication of how many lives he had touched.

Because of his seemingly greater popularity, people who knew him frequently refer to Sister Eric Marie as "Ed's sister the sister."

I was having an especially difficult day when I first realized the unique gifts possessed by Ed's sister the sister. I bumped into her in a campus hallway, which led to a conversation that ultimately ended with me asking her to come and speak to the team. This team was an exceptionally difficult group, and I figured if I was not getting through to them, maybe she could. What did I have to lose? This became the first of many occasions that I had her speak to the team.

My conversation that day in the hallway with Sister Eric Marie started the same way that her conversations with all troubled souls usually go. With a warm and friendly expression on her face, she looks the person in the eye, tilts her head ever so slightly, and asks, "Are you all right?" Most people, myself included, brush the question off and respond with the expected stock answer of "I'm fine," well aware that it's not the truth.

She usually accepts the answer and probes no further. Inevitably, though, she will circle back and ask the question again. "Are you all right?" It may take a few sentences, or even a few days or weeks, but she always poses it again. The next time she asks, it is hard to give the same stock reply as before. It seems dishonest to do so. She is so talented at establishing almost instant rapport, and comes across as so trustworthy, that people feel guilty telling her they are fine when they know they are not. It is in that moment of truth that the floodgates generally open up.

Sister Eric Marie came and talked to the entire team during our next study hall session. I excused myself from the room and gave her carte blanche with the players. I still have no idea what she talked about that day, nor what the players divulged. All I know is that the players ate it up, and she apparently connected with them.

It naturally got me thinking—what was she doing that I was not? Why were they so receptive to her and so willing to drop their guard in her presence? Whatever she was doing made her a better coach than me. My knowledge of Xs and Os may have exceeded hers, but Sister Eric Marie's ability to connect with the players put me to shame. In terms of getting the players to learn to be good teammates, her skills were far more valuable than mine.

Although Sister Eric Marie enjoyed sports and played them in her younger days, she has never really been a coach. Similar to how the unorthodox coaching backgrounds of Burt, Dennis Gibson, and Tim Kelly caused them to think and act outside the confines of traditional coaching models, Sister Eric Marie's background presumably did the same.

To someone unfamiliar with the structure of the Catholic Church, I suppose the concept of being a nun could be confusing. Technically, Sister Eric Marie is not a nun, she's a sister. The term "sister" and "nun" are commonly used interchangeably, and I've even heard her refer to herself with both words—but there is a difference. The commonality is that sisters and nuns are both Catholic women who give their lives to the service of God by taking vows of poverty, chastity, and obedience.[47] Although they take vows, they are not ordained members of the clergy and do not perform Catholic mass, as priests do.[48] They are part of the laity.

The primary difference between nuns and sisters is that nuns live a contemplative, cloistered life. They spend their time working and praying inside the confines of a monastery or convent. Sisters are more active and visible in their ministries. They tend to serve the interests of people in need through a variety of different work outside their convents.[49] The fact that both sisters and nuns dress very modestly and that both are addressed as "Sister" makes the distinction confusing.

In either case, these women always belong to a religious order, such as the Carmelites, the Franciscans, or the Sisters of St. Joseph. Sister Eric Marie belongs to the order of the Religious Sisters of Mercy.

Founded in Dublin, Ireland in 1831 by Catherine McAuley, the Sisters of Mercy are deeply devoted to their vows. The story of the order's origin is fascinating in its own right. When McAuley's parents died at an early age, a wealthy Protestant couple welcomed her into their home. She served as a companion and household manager for the elderly couple who had no children of their own. Upon their death, she inherited their entire estate.

The generous nature of the couple and their commitment to charitable causes always moved McAuley. She made a decision to use her inheritance to build a house on Baggot Street in Dublin to educate and shelter destitute girls. The House of Mercy, as it was called, became the foundation of her religious order. Initially, her neighbors met her new project with criticism. One reason was the location of the house. Baggot Street was a historically upper-class neighborhood in those days. Another reason was that people could not understand her motives and questioned why these women were doing the work of the clergy.[50]

The Archbishop of Dublin, however, was impressed with the ministry that was taking place at the House of Mercy and advised McAuley to consider starting a more formal religious congregation. That suggestion led to the birth of the Sisters of Mercy.[51] They continue to minister to the needy and embrace the same core values, but they have grown considerably since the House of Mercy days. The Sisters of Mercy now operate hospitals, orphanages, and schools all over the world. Mount Aloysius College happens to be one of 17 Mercy institutions of higher education in the United States.[52]

Sister Eric Marie became a sister when she was 24, which made her decisively older than most of the other women who entered the convent at that time. The majority of them were still teenagers and just barely out of high school. She was comparatively more experienced in the ways of the world, and she had tasted adult life before taking her vows.

When a sister enters the convent, she traditionally adopts a new name. It is symbolic of her entering a new life. There are several occasions in the Bible when people are given different names for the same reason. In John 1:42, Jesus gave Simon the name Peter. In the book of Genesis, Abram became Abraham and Sarai became Sarah. In keeping with this practice, the Sisters of Mercy ask their candidates to take a new name when they accept their vows.

Sister Eric Marie was born Marcella Lucille Setlock. She chose the name Eric Marie with the help of her father, with whom she was very close. His name was Edward Setlock, and she wanted to show homage to him by choosing the name Edward. Unfortunately, there were already so many variations of Edward in the order that she was inclined to pick something else.

While going through a book of names, her father suggested Eric. When she read that the meaning of the name meant "strong," she thought it to be appropriate, since her early days in the convent were more challenging than she had expected. The name Marie was added, as many sisters attach a form of Mary to their name. She told me one of the most touching moments of her life was the day her Mother Superior called her in and told her she would now be known as Sister Eric Marie in Heaven.

I always found it ironic that Sister Eric Marie is viewed as a religious figure because she does not fit into any religious stereotype that I know of. She is not judgmental nor self-righteous, and she never forces her faith on anyone. I once had a non-Catholic recruit visit the campus. He loved our team, how we played, and all of the other basketball-related aspects. But as we were giving him his tour, I could tell that the statues and other religious icons around campus made him uneasy. We finally got back to the gym, a place where he felt comfortable, and Sister Eric Marie came walking around the corner.

I thought to myself that the sight of a nun will just about put the nail in this recruit's coffin. Sister Eric Marie began talking to him, and the recruit suddenly blurted out that he's not Catholic, like it had been brewing inside of him and he couldn't contain it any longer. Sister Eric Marie chuckled, leaned in and touched his arm, and said, "Oh, that's okay, honey. That doesn't matter." The recruit smiled; she had put his reservations to rest.

Her open approach most certainly stems from her upbringing. She was raised in the small western Pennsylvania coal-mining town of McIntyre where, like everyone else in town, her universe revolved around three things—the coal mine, the school, and the church. Although she was raised Catholic, she never attended parochial school and she is hesitant to label her family as overly religious.

Her father worked in the coal mines, as did most every other man in the community. He came from a large family, which was common in those days. He was the eighth of eleven children. Sister Eric Marie recalls he was a big influence on the neighborhood kids. Boys were always sitting with her father on the front porch, seeking his advice and treating him like a surrogate father.

Her mother also came from a large family, with six brothers and three sisters. Together, her parents raised three children of their own—Catherine, Marcella (Sister Eric Marie), and Buddy. By her account, Sister Eric Marie grew up in a loving, supportive home.

When she graduated from high school, she took the less conventional route. Most of her friends were getting married and starting families. She chose, instead, to go to college. In due course, she graduated with a degree in music education from the State Teacher's College at Indiana. The school would later change its name to the Indiana University of Pennsylvania.[53]

After completing college, she took a job as a music teacher at Cresson Joint High School. At an early age, she demonstrated a gift for dealing with troubled young men. During her first year, the principal assigned her a class comprised of fifteen of the school's most difficult boys. They were problem kids for everyone else, yet she seemed to tame them with ease.

After a few years of teaching, she found herself facing a dilemma. She had started dating a young man whom she liked very much. At the same time, the first love of her life came back into the picture, and she found herself confronted with choosing which one to marry. She did the only thing she could think of—she prayed, hoping God would provide her with the answer she needed.

She viewed the institution of marriage as sacred and wanted to be sure to get it right. Then, one afternoon while walking home and thinking about her dilemma, she broke down crying because she knew the answer: neither of them. In her moment of despondency, she experienced the onset of what is commonly referred to as a calling. *Why don't you become a nun?* Trying to explain a calling to someone who has never had the experience is next to impossible.

Not long before her moment of enlightenment, she had met a sister who was teaching music at nearby Mount Aloysius College. Under the guise of getting to know the sister better and learning more about an upcoming concert, she made a call and arranged a meeting. Her ulterior motive was to inquire what becoming a nun entailed. Serendipitously, the day she knocked on the door of Mount Aloysius happened to be the Feast of Our Lady of Mercy—a special celebratory occasion for the Sisters of Mercy. She saw it as a sign from above and she decided to move forward with this new plan.

Her father and mother were saddened by the news, but they were supportive. When she told her boyfriend of her decision, she got an equally favorable response. He told her that he understood and didn't think he could compete with *that* guy anyway. He also joked that he wasn't going to try to talk her out of it because God might strike him down.

With the blessings of her friends and family in tow, she set off for the Sisters of Mercy convent. It was not an easy transition. Her experience was not entirely different from that of Maria in *The Sound of Music*.[54] Sister Eric Marie liked to sing and dance and loved life to the fullest. She would often get scolded for singing or being too loud in the convent. Living a subdued, monastic lifestyle was a challenge for her, and she questioned what she was doing on more than a few occasions.

Once, she walked outside to find one of her friends from the convent agonizing over the same issues she was having. It was a Friday night, with the sounds of the marching band from the local high school football game playing in the background, her friend confided in her that all she wanted was a cigarette and a return to the comforts of her old life.

Fortunately for me, they consoled each other and persevered, convincing themselves they were in the right place and seeking the right purpose. Equally fortunate is that they had good mentors at the convent—experienced sisters who showed them compassion and supported them in their moments of uncertainty. This is ideally how good teammates provide a support system for one another.

When Sister Eric Marie finished her training, she returned to Mount Aloysius where she would serve the needs of the students and the community for the better part of the next 40 years. Interestingly, the friend who craved a cigarette on that regretful Friday night went on to become a beloved member of the Board of Trustees at Mount Aloysius. And the boyfriend Sister Eric Marie left behind, waited and remained unmarried the entire time she was in training to become a sister. He married someone else the year after she took her final vows. All of them continue to be close friends to this day.

In the convent, the new sisters were asked to do a number of menial tasks, like cleaning. Their organization had the means to pay someone to do these tasks, which would potentially have allowed the sisters in training more time to focus exclusively on their theological studies, but it wouldn't have necessarily made them better sisters. Doing the mundane, menial tasks was exhausting at times, but it gave the sisters an appreciation for the workload and psyche of the type of people they would potentially encounter and to whom they would have to minister when their training was complete.

It did something else, too. It gave them a sense of belonging, knowing that every sister who had come before them had engaged in this same humbling work. No member of the Sisters of Mercy was ever elevated to exalted status without first traveling this path, and that is something they all took pride in knowing. This sense of community was a strong bond.

A similar situation of entitlement often plays out with sports teams. There are menial tasks to be done—sweeping the court, doing the laundry, carrying the equipment, etc.—and also the means to have them done by people other than the players. Having someone else do these tasks would potentially allow the players more time to focus on their sports skills, but it wouldn't necessarily make them better teammates.

If a coach is serious about building good teammates, then this is an area that should get attention. On our team, we used to make the freshman carry the bags and have the managers do all of the other stuff. Looking back, it was mild rookie hazing and encouraged upperclassman entitlement. Now, we do it much differently. We have an almost ceremonial event where all newcomers, be it freshman or transfers, are assigned their official "job."

I compile a list of essential, yet menial, jobs that need to be done. Some of them are ordinary things like laundry and carrying the equipment bags on and off the bus, but some of the jobs are unique to our program's priorities. For instance, we have one player assigned to go through the locker room after an away game and make sure every ounce of trash is picked up and the room is left in as perfect a state as possible. We have another player assigned to be the last person off the bus when we travel to away games. His job is to make sure all of the trash is thrown away and that nothing is left behind on the bus.

When it comes time to give out the job assignments, we always gather the team together for a special night. We order pizza and wings and the entire team watches the movie *Hoosiers* together— hence this event is customarily dubbed "Hoosier Night." When the movie is over, I write each of the necessary jobs on the board, and the veteran players hand out the assignments to the newcomers.

After all of the duties have been assigned, I explain to the newcomers exactly what their new job entails and the significance it plays within our team. I then go around the room and randomly ask returning players what their job used to be. I get responses like, "I was a floor sweeper" or "I was a laundryman." At that moment, the newcomers get a sense that they are part of something bigger than themselves. They gain the appreciation that they are not the first ones to go down this road.

I let the veteran players assign the jobs at their discretion and deliberately do not interfere with their selections. The only caveat is that the newcomer assigned to a job must be trained by the teammate who previously held that job. Which means that the laundryman from the last season, who is now a sophomore, is responsible for teaching the freshman laundryman exactly how the laundry is supposed to be done. If the practice gear is still wet for the start of practice, then the sophomore who was supposed to train the freshman how to do the laundry is just as responsible for the failure as the freshman. For that matter, the senior who trained the junior, and the junior who trained the sophomore, are also complicit if the freshman fails in his duties. The teammates take ownership of the job and pride in seeing it done correctly.

They are being trained to be good teammates in a way that has nothing to do with their athletic abilities. On a side note, there is a mutual benefit to this arrangement. Our team managers have the time to do other more impactful things like compile stats since they are not asked to do all of the menial labor tasks. Also, we no longer have to worry about players accidently leaving their phones or wallets on the bus. The last player off the bus catches all of that now. It is a classic "Burt" win/win scenario.

Mount Aloysius was not always co-ed. The college itself has an interesting history. When Catherine McAuley died in 1841, she had already branched out with several other establishments in addition to her House of Mercy in Dublin. Two years after her death, the first Irish Sisters of Mercy arrived in the United States by way of an invitation from the Bishop of Pittsburgh.[55]

Five years later, Mother Frances Warde, who had founded the first American convent, sent sisters to the mountains east of Pittsburgh to establish a convent in the village of Loretto, Pennsylvania. The sisters set up a school in a tinsmith's shop upon their arrival in Loretto, which was the forerunner to what came to be known as St. Aloysius Academy. There is some debate over what year Mount Aloysius was founded. Saint Aloysius Academy was built in 1853. Some use that date as the establishment of Mount Aloysius. However, the location of Saint Aloysius Academy was moved to its present site in 1897. It was renamed Mount Aloysius Junior College in 1939, and others choose to use that date as the beginning of the college.[56]

Mount Aloysius remained a women-only junior college until the late 60s. Sister Eric Marie arrived at the school during the transitional period, and she can still remember the names of the male students from those first classes. The College amended its charter again in 1991 and offered bachelor's degrees. The word "Junior" was dropped from its name shortly after that.

Before there were organized intercollegiate teams at Mount Aloysius, the male students used to play basketball in the tiny multi-purpose room that doubled as a theater and a gymnasium near Sister Eric Marie's office. Whenever students got hurt, they would come to see her because she had the first aid kit. While I am sure the bandages she issued were helpful, I suspect it was her warm and caring attention that actually healed what was ailing them.

The other sisters at Mount Aloysius seemed to me to be cut from a different fabric than Sister Eric Marie when I started working there. They were difficult and mean-spirited—or so I thought at the time. The vice president of the college was Virginia Bertschi, or Sister Ginny, as she was more commonly known. Sister Ginny was a large woman, and she was one tough cookie. She ruled with an iron fist and kept an iron clamp on the college's purse strings.

We were trying to build the athletic program, and she sometimes made it difficult. My coaching friends would ask me what it was like to work for the nuns at Mount Aloysius. I would tell them it was like being asked to dig a six-foot-deep ditch the length of the campus. If I had a backhoe, it would have it done in a few days. If I had a shovel, I'd have it done in a few months. But I was given a spoon, and every so often they come around wanting to know why the ditch wasn't done yet. No matter what answer I gave, they shook their heads in disappointment. And then Sister Ginny would kick a little dirt back in the ditch before she walked away, just to reinforce her disappointment in my progress.

There is no shortage of Sister Ginny stories at Mount Aloysius. I was asked to sit in on a construction meeting once for a campus renovation project that was behind schedule. I was stunned by how Sister Ginny put the contractors and architects in their place. Her language and tone surpassed that of any sailor I'd ever met. Make no mistake about it, she had complete control over that meeting.

Another time, we were trying to spruce up our make-shift athletic training room. It didn't have any storage cabinets and we needed more training tables. The proposal we submitted to purchase those items was promptly denied. These were things we needed, so I volunteered to build them myself if the college paid for the materials.

I went to the local lumber yard, bought what we needed and then built the cabinets and the tables in my garage with my tools. I tried to keep the costs down and chose lesser-quality wood. They didn't turn out to be showroom-caliber, but they met our needs.

After the cabinets were completed and installed, I turned in a receipt for reimbursement of the materials I had purchased. The next day, I got a call from Sister Ginny, wanting to know why I bought such expensive screws. Not, "Thank you." Not, "How did the cabinets turn out?" Nothing along those lines. She was only worried about the costs of the screws.

Being around Sister Eric Marie has caused me to see Sister Ginny and all of the other sisters who used to frustrate me through different eyes, and I now understand. It was about their mission. In addition to the three vows of poverty, chastity, and obedience, Sisters of Mercy take a fourth vow of service to the poor, sick, and uneducated.[57]

Sister Ginny was fond of saying, "Without the means, there can be no mission." I always thought it was her way of justifying being overly thrifty. Now I understand that wasn't what she was saying. The money I could have saved by buying cheaper screws didn't go to line her pockets, it went to advance the mission. It was spent on financing orphanages, educating kids, and paying to operate hospitals for sick people who couldn't otherwise afford it without the Sisters' help. Those women did important work, and every penny counted.

I was speaking at a coach's clinic one year and I made a joke about the Sisters' frugality. There was a vendor in the lobby whose company manufactured uniforms. I was trying to plug his company and the quality of his product. I joked to the audience that his uniforms are made to last. I followed that up by saying, "I work for nuns. They've worn the same clothes since 1960, and they expect our team to do so too. That's why we have to buy uniforms that last."

I feel so guilty ever thinking that way. It is a tremendous sacrifice the sisters make to dress so modestly, and why they do it should have tugged a little harder at my heartstrings. They are frugal for incredibly honorable reasons. I was regrettably too self-centered to comprehend the depths of their sacrifice.

Todd Henry is the founder and CEO of Accidental Creative, a consultancy that helps people and organizations tap into their creative side to generate what he calls "brilliant" ideas. In his book *Die Empty: Unleash Your Best Work Every Day*, he mentions that, as a conversation starter, he likes to pose the question, "If you could snap your fingers right now and make anything happen in your job, what would it be?"

The answers typically fall into two distinct categories—contingency and ownership. The first group feels their success is contingent upon the removal of some constraint that holds them back. This could be a tight budget, an unappreciative boss, or a policy that is not in line with their goals. The second group tends to take personal responsibility for their own success, and they want greater and different responsibilities within the organization. In essence, they are owners of the problem, not victims.[58]

In my pre-Sister Eric Marie days, I was clearly in the contingency category. I saw my job at Mount Aloysius as a means to an end. The confines I perceived to exist made me bitter and frustrated. She enabled me to change my perspective and become a facilitator of the Sisters' mission instead. Once I embraced this, it was impossible to go back to feeling the same way.

I noticed I developed new behavior. If I was walking through campus and saw a weed growing through the sidewalk, I pulled it out. I didn't point out that maintenance was not doing their job or worry about whose fault it was that the weed was allowed to grow that high. If I walked by the gym, and the lights were on and nobody was in there, I turned them off. I wanted our college's electric bill to be lower. It wasn't only pride, it was the first step in the discovery of purpose and becoming a good teammate.

Sister Ginny had a purpose and a role within the mission. She was a protector. If she was abrasive, it was because she was trying to protect the capacity for the mission to continue to move forward. The emotion attached to protective action is unlike anything else. Think of a mother bear and her cub. If her cub's safety is threatened, the mother bear will act differently. It's not self-preservation, it is the preservation of something greater than self. The mission was Sister Ginny's life, and she perpetually operated within the margins of her protective instincts.

As I learned from Sister Eric Marie, I also had a purpose and it was different from what I had originally thought. Like the vast majority of coaches, I believed my purpose was to represent the university by winning games and conducting myself in an honorable fashion. But that is only a small part of your job when you work for the Sisters of Mercy. Embracing the mission and having genuine purpose goes beyond that.

My purpose was to help advance the mission and serve the needs of the players. To me, that meant teaching the players to be good teammates. In many regards, I was not that much different than a physician who worked for a Sisters of Mercy-owned hospital. The physician served the needs of the mission by helping the sick, but he also served the needs of his patients by making them feel better.

At some point, while researching the history of the Sisters of Mercy, it occurred to me that being a good teammate and satisfying all three components of the definition was largely about effectively applying the Mercy values—mercy, justice, hospitality, and service—to the team. Those values are derived directly from the vows the sisters take.

While writing this book, I experienced more than a few restless nights contemplating what content should be included and what course the story should take. It was during those times that I unavoidably came across a magazine article or late night television show that sparked an idea and led to the end of my writing paralysis. One of those incidents happened while channel surfing and landing on a C-Span2 broadcast of an interview with Robert Grenier, the former Director of the CIA Counter-Terrorism Center, who recently authored the book *88 Days to Kandahar: A CIA Diary.*

In the spirit of full disclosure, I have never read Grenier's book, nor is it the kind of reading that normally piques my interest. However, during the television interview I happened upon, he told an interesting story about advice he had received from an older colleague when he first started working for the CIA concerning the political landscape of the spy business. The veteran mentor told him always to remember, "Fear drives the system."[59]

The fear he was talking about was political fallout. People are scared of potential violence, and that's why they invest time and resources. Congressmen and other political leaders fear potential backlash, should the public find out that acts of violence happened because elected officials refused to allocate sufficient funds that could have prevented the travesty. Politicians have an aversion to being blamed for disasters. Fear drives the system.

In many ways, this is also true of organized sports, in that the fear of *losing* drives the system. Coaches push players towards competitiveness and emphasize winning above what will make a difference in their players' future. Coaches push because they are fearful of losing—losing their jobs, losing respect, and so on. Athletic administrations demand victories from coaches because they are afraid of the potential backlash that could occur if the public perceives that the losses happened because of something the administrations failed to manage adequately.

The final chapters of this book focus on applying the values of the Sisters of Mercy to strategies that build good teammates and to finding an alternative to fear to drive the coaching system.

10

USING MERCY TO BUILD GOOD TEAMMATES

ONE of my biggest concerns in writing this book was that the idea of building good teammates could be misconstrued as a socialistic attempt to muddy the waters of individualism and flatten nonconformist behavior—i.e., to make everyone on the team behave exactly the same. Nothing could be further from the truth. Good teams have diversity and the variety of personalities, beliefs, and principles of its members are what makes the team stronger than any individual.

Each member of a team brings a unique gift to the group, and building good teammates is about helping players appreciate where their unique gifts fit into the context of the team and how they can use their gifts for the betterment of the entire group. If players grasp this concept while participating in sports, they will be able to capitalize on it when they enter the workforce.

It is the namesake value of the Sisters of Mercy that allows coaches to teach individuals to do this. I asked Sister Eric Marie what "mercy" was, and she instinctively turned the question back to me and responded, "What do *you* think mercy is?"

To be honest, I wasn't entirely sure how to answer her. When I think of mercy, the first thing that comes to mind is a medieval executioner with a black hood and an ax, standing over a condemned man, while chants of "Mercy!" echo from the onlooking crowd. Or perhaps, it is a last-minute phone call from the governor staying the execution of a death row inmate. To me, that is mercy.

When I told Sister Eric Marie my thoughts, she replied, "Oh, it's more than just that."

I took another stab and suggested it was a judge handing down a lighter sentence than what was deserved. Again, she replied, "Oh, it's more than just that."

We went a few more rounds like that until I was finally brought to the conclusion that mercy is an all-encompassing term for kindness. It is treating someone with compassion when you could have rightly treated them with harshness. This is precisely how good teammates should act toward their fellow teammates.

As a coach, it is natural to cast judgment on players. Some would argue that this is the very essence of coaching—identifying faults and devising plans to eliminate them. Maybe it is, but the timing of doing so can make all the difference regarding how well the recommendations are received. Sister Eric Marie has a motto for dealing with new acquaintances and the necessity to defer judgment: *Take them where they are.*

It is not so much a statement on assessment as it is seeing the potential and possessing empathy. *Take them where they are* is about accepting the hand a person was dealt and embracing the challenge of helping him reach his full potential through merciful actions. It is not about passing judgment and dismissing people because they start off at a less-than-convenient place in life.

As an undergrad, I had a theater history class in which the professor explained to us the notion that a play is only a blip in time. It is not the whole story. Plenty happens before the story begins, and there is plenty that happens after the story ends. There is a background and history to why the Capulets hate the Montagues. Shakespeare only tells part of the story in *Romeo and Juliet*; we join the story already in progress.

Whenever a coach meets a player for the first time, the temptation is to form an opinion without considering the depth of the player's backstory. If this temptation exists for coaches, then it is amplified tenfold for the player's teammates. Coaches have to find a way to get the team to appreciate where the new player is coming from, including the origins of his opinions, speech patterns, and wardrobe. There is a tendency for players to distance themselves from new teammates who do not fit into the current culture of the team.

The military is notorious for stripping down new recruits to a common base and forcing the institution's will upon them. The recruit has no choice but to fit in. As soon as a new Marine arrives at Parris Island for boot camp, he is stripped of his civilian clothes, has his head shaved, and is indoctrinated into a new way of doing things. While this may work for the Marine Corps, any semblance of this "strip down" methodology has become increasingly more challenging to incorporate into sports training. Because of things like video games, social media, and the Internet, there are too many alternative activities and entertainment options for a Millennial to choose from.

If you were to take a hardline approach now, it would not be surprising for a player to walk away. You could say that player was not tough enough or worthy enough to live up to the team's standards, but what good does that do? Ultimately, the goal is to become an inclusive entity that uses sports as a means to teach young people social intangibles like being a good teammate. If players aren't present, they can't be taught.

I used to gather my team for a meeting at the beginning of the season and make a big deal out of laying down the laws of the land. "Get your earrings out. Get your hair cut. Get your shirts tucked in." There may be genuine value to having those kinds of standards in place, but now, based largely on Sister Eric Marie's advice, I don't approach it that way. I give players a much longer grace period before we even discuss these standards. It is an exercise in patience and temporary tolerance.

There is a teacher at my daughter's school who takes a similar approach with her students. She doesn't assign them seats for the first few weeks of the school year. She lets the students sit beside their friends and allows them to become comfortable with their new surroundings. Having elementary students sit in assigned seats can understandably produce strategic results. They are organized. They have fewer distractions in the classroom. They are separated from their friends, significantly reducing the chance for them to be chatty instead of paying attention to the teacher.

However, immediately implementing that strategy may not produce the best results in the long run. It plays into the coaching precept, "They don't care what you know until they know you care." Sure, setting the tone early and assigning seats will establish an environment more structured and conducive to learning. But showing patience and offering an early grace period to allow students to be themselves and get acclimated to their new surroundings creates trust and a level of comfort.

This particular teacher may have gotten off to a slower start in perceived classroom organization and controlled teaching opportunities, but by the end of the school year, her students routinely demonstrated higher degrees of learning, and she was regularly recognized as one of the school district's most beloved teachers. I believe how she handled the beginning of the school year built greater rapport with her students and led to her higher rate of success.

Interestingly, that delay often eliminates the need to even have such a formal rule-setting session. When you show mercy early, new players frequently adopt the standards on their own without being told to do so. They become more observant of their veteran teammates and more accepting of the standards, not because they are forced to follow, but because they want to be included. They see their inclusion as a more prominent factor in the establishment of their identity, and they take ownership of the standards.

Sister Eric Marie's belief of not shaming players with discipline is closely related to her concept of "take them where they are." It is easy for a coach to unintentionally allow this to happen. A player makes an error in practice or in a game and you lambast him right on the spot. You justify it to yourself as "seizing the teachable moment," and you try to make such a profound impact that he will be unlikely ever to repeat the mistake. You're not only sending a message to that player but also to any teammates observing you.

Your intentions are admirable, but this approach can do serious damage to how his teammates view the player, which can hinder his capacity to be a good teammate. By singling him out so dramatically, you inadvertently turn him into an individual. You ostracize him from the team. He will inevitably go into fight or flight mode, and neither one encourages him to put the needs of the team ahead of his own.

Recently, I had a player curse out an assistant coach during practice. The player was upset by how critical the coach was and voiced his dissatisfaction. No matter how you looked at it, the player was wrong. I understood why the player was emotional, but his actions were completely unacceptable. You cannot allow players to speak to coaches like that.

My initial instinct was to immediately halt practice and tear into the player. I wanted to make an example of him. I wanted to put him on the line and make him run sprints or maybe even something worse. The thing was, this player happened to be our best student. He was a presidential scholar with a near-perfect grade point average and our senior captain. The other players respected him for being a model player on and off the court. This type of transgression was out of character for him.

When I heard the player go off on the assistant coach, I contained my instinctive reaction and decided to adhere to the Sister Eric Marie maxim of not shaming players with discipline. It was as if a miniature nun magically appeared on my shoulder and whispered the word "mercy" in my ear. I heard what the player said to the assistant coach, but I decided to ignore it and did my best to move onto the next drill as quickly and smoothly as possible.

This was a risky move because there were other variables to consider. How would the other players perceive my not reacting to what happened? What about the assistant coach? I wasn't sure how the assistant coach was going to respond. He was the one who was directly disrespected and whose authority was called into question. I advise assistant coaches and players to be more concerned with finding a way to earn a person's respect than with wasting energy worrying about being disrespected. Fortunately, the assistant coach heeded my advice in this instance and followed my lead in moving on to the next drill.

The player's words were loud enough for most of the players and me to hear. But there was other activity going on in the gym and not everyone saw what happened. The outburst wasn't bad enough to totally disrupt practice or for the gym to come to a complete standstill.

My primary concern was that if I came down too hard on the player, he would be humiliated and embarrassed to the point that he would have to defend his honor or jeopardize losing face in front of the other players. As he was the team's captain, I didn't want to undermine his authority or create a situation where the respect he had from the other players was put in jeopardy. I made the decision to hold off and address this issue with him in private, away from the other members of the team. I pretended not to hear what he said.

After practice, I pulled the assistant coach aside and talked to him about what had happened. I thanked him for his patience and applauded his restraint. I also explained to him my plan to handle the situation.

I waited until the end of practice the next day. This gave everyone's emotions plenty of time to subside. When the team gathered together, I gave my usual final comments and then casually—but in front of the team—asked the player who confronted the assistant coach the previous day, if he would hang back and meet with me in my office for a few minutes.

After the court had cleared, the player, the assistant coach, and I sat down in my office. I explained how disappointed I was with what had happened. He was an intelligent kid, so I didn't need to patronize him by stating why it was wrong. He understood. I asked him if there was anything he wanted to say, and he explained himself and apologized to the assistant coach and me for his outburst.

He apologized to the team at the start of the next day's practice. I had not asked him to apologize. He made the decision on his own and that resulted in it coming across as sincere. I think the other players respected him even more for apologizing and owning

137

up to his mistake. They understood his frustration and his uncharacteristic lapse in judgment. His sincerity strengthened the bond he had with his teammates.

The mercy I showed him allowed the player to continue to focus on learning to be a good teammate. He wasn't polarized with emotion. I didn't shame him. I took into account his past actions and his earned reputation. We corrected the problem and did our best to prevent repeated offenses.

It was sufficient that the other players heard me ask him to stay behind and talk in my office. They knew what it was about. Players talk to each other. After the player and I spoke, I'm sure he went to his dorm and told his teammates about the conversation.

It is worth mentioning that as concerned as I was with the undermining of this player's authority, I was just as concerned with the undermining of the assistant coach's authority—and mine too. In the end, I decided it was easier for the assistant coach and me to re-establish authority than it would have been for the player to re-establish his authority as captain. I had the luxury of exerting my authority in any number of different ways; the player did not. In the grand scheme of things, and with regard to building good teammates, this player's relationship with his teammates was more important than my perceived lack of authority. Sometimes having mercy is knowing what to ignore.

There was another time when I failed to assert mercy when disciplining a player, and the repercussions of that failure continue to haunt me. We had a player who was not going to class. I am realistic in that I do not expect all of our players to get perfect grades, but I do expect them to make an effort and actually attend their classes. I tried talking to this player about his absenteeism, but it didn't work. He continued to miss class.

This player had an unusual background. While he was in high school, he was caught stealing his stepfather's car, and due in large part to the stepfather's recommendation, the judge sent him to a reform school for juvenile delinquents. He had good size and talent. However, because of his troubled past, a lot of bigger schools steered clear of him. A former player of mine was working as a counselor at the reform school and had vouched for the changes this kid had made in his life. The counselor believed the player was capable of making it in college if someone would just give him a chance.

At first, the player was a little rough around the edges, but he was coming around. But then the issue of him missing class surfaced. I tried calling him before each of his classes. I tried having another player knock on his door before class. I even went to his dorm room and literally walked him to his classes. Eventually, I convinced myself that I was doing him a disservice by coddling him too much, so I decided it was time to put an end to his attendance problem once and for all.

I told him to meet me in the gym tomorrow morning. I had intended to discipline him in such a way that he would never want to miss class again. I was going to make him do "towel suicides" until he got the point. This is an extremely grueling exercise, where the player has to run a series of sprints while pushing a towel along the court floor. The player has to bend over and get low to the ground in an almost-crawling position. For a big guy like this player, it is exhausting. Our season had already ended, so it wasn't like I could withhold playing time by benching him or anything like that. I thought this was the best way to bring about corrective action.

When he showed up at the gym and saw what I had in store for him, he was not thrilled. He took about three steps and then threw down his towel and declared he wasn't doing this. I argued with him for a few seconds and then told him either he does it or there's the door. He chose to quit and walk away. As he was leaving, I recall saying to him something along the lines of, "You are going to regret it if you walk out that door." He left anyway, and that was the last real interaction I ever had with him.

A couple of years later, I got an email from someone asking me if I had heard about this player. They sent me a link to a YouTube video of the player appearing on an episode of the *Bill Cunningham Show*—a Maury Povich/Jerry Springer-style syndicated television program. In the video, the host reads the results of a lie detector test and it is revealed that the player lied about physically abusing his girlfriend, and she lied about deliberately blowing marijuana smoke into their nine-month-old daughter's face.

Watching the video was heartbreaking. The player was not being a good teammate when he chose to miss class. He couldn't grasp that his actions affected the reputation of the entire team, not to mention that his becoming academically ineligible would have had tremendous ramifications on the team's potential success on the court. He was acting selfishly by not going to class. It was clear in the video that he was not being a good teammate to his new team either—his family.

I had good intentions in trying to get the player to go to class. But my choice in disciplining him lacked mercy, and it had a ripple effect on this young man's life. He made his own choices and had arrived at that unfortunate spot as a result of those decisions. Perhaps I could have prevented that from occurring and altered the course of his life if I had only shown more mercy.

I should have worried less about his eligibility and academic problems and focused on the primary objective of teaching him to be a good teammate. There were a thousand other ways I could have handled the situation and achieved that lesson. I could have continued to coddle him and walk him to classes. I could have enlisted the assistance of more outside help. I could have even let him fail his classes and become ineligible. In time, all of those could have brought about the necessary change that would have prevented him from arriving at that ill-fated place.

Players have to be held accountable, and they must understand there are consequences to their actions. However, the path by which they reach those consequences can make all the difference. Sometimes mercy means having the willingness to step into someone else's shoes and having the courage to see things through that person's eyes. When leaders are able to do this, they connect with players in a way that allows for the building of good teammates.

11

USING JUSTICE TO BUILD GOOD TEAMMATES

IF you are in the coaching profession long enough, you will encounter times when players run afoul of expectations. When you're done dealing with these situations, the important thing is not to hold it against the player. Mercy is as much about forgiveness and "letting things go" as anything else. If you allow the remnants of an offense to hover over the player, his teammates will pick up on it, and it may prevent them from fully accepting the player back into their good graces. He will have a hard time becoming a good teammate under those circumstances.

This is where the Sisters of Mercy value of "justice" comes into play. Sister Eric Marie is capable of wiping a slate clean more quickly than anyone I've ever met. For that matter, this is a skill that all of the Sisters of Mercy whom I have encountered seem to possess. One of the only disagreements Sister Eric Marie and I ever had revolved around the issue of justice.

We had a former Mount Aloysius player arrested for selling drugs. It wasn't just any player, either. This particular person was well known. He had finished his career as one of the college's all-time statistical leaders. His arrest was very public, and he was prosecuted in federal court because he was arrested for selling crack near a playground.

He played at the college before I was hired, so I never coached him, although I had interacted with him on many occasions and knew who he was. As the college's current coach, I saw myself as the caretaker of the basketball program, and I made the decision to have the plaque commemorating the player's accomplishments removed from our trophy case.

This did not sit well with Sister Eric Marie. She never told me not to remove the plaque, but a blind man could see her disapproval—and it ate at me for months. I felt the trophy case was a place of distinction, reserved for those who had conducted themselves honorably. I didn't feel as though this player had done that. Sister Eric Marie saw it differently.

What I was unaware of was that she had been visiting this player in prison and counseling him. She had also attended the court proceedings with his family. She saw another side of him and his situation. From Sister Eric Marie's perspective, justice didn't mean condoning the infraction. It meant getting those who did wrong to see the error in what they did and getting them to make amends.

In this case, the player had become involved in a bad lifestyle because he wanted his sons to have the best clothes and the nicest shoes. Dealing drugs was a means for him to achieve that objective. In theory, he had good intentions, in that he was thinking of his team—his family. You could say he was caring about his teammates because his motivation was the needs of his sons. You could also say he was sharing because of how he spent the money he made.

Where he failed, however, was that he didn't listen to what his teammates were actually saying to him. Sister Eric Marie convinced him that his sons didn't want the nicest shoes, they wanted his time and his attention. That was what was important and that was what he needed to hear.

On a side note, perhaps my favorite Sister Eric Marie story involved an experience she had while visiting this player inside the prison. Something happened that sent the facility into lockdown. In a perceivably tense and perilous situation, she managed to stay quite calm. Suspecting that she could be masking her concern, the player reassured her, saying, "Don't worry, Sister; I got you. Nothing's going to happen to you while I'm here." His attempt to calm her and his willingness to protect her gave insight to the kind of person he was deep down.

I eventually, and rightfully, came around to Sister Eric Marie's way of thinking and put the player's plaque back in the trophy case. As coaches, we invest a lot of effort in getting players to be loyal to the team, and we expect them to be there when the team needs them. That loyalty needs to be reciprocated, and sometimes the team must be there for the player, even if that player has long exhausted his eligibility.

I took the plaque away because I thought it sent the wrong message to our current students. I should have kept it there because it was sending the right message to the player in question. He needed to be reminded that he was once, figuratively, on top of the world, and with the right changes, he could be there again. That plaque was a reminder not to lose hope. Keeping it in the trophy case was a way for the team to be there for him.

I am happy to report that he turned his life around since being released from prison. He has become a fantastic father. He is deeply involved in his children's lives in a very positive way. The sacrifices he continues to make on their behalf are paying dividends. He also willingly shares his experiences with other young people and mentors them so they don't make the same mistakes that he did. If all of this isn't enough, he also has found a way to give back to the community by volunteering and helping to organize his hometown's most successful AAU basketball program.

Unfortunately, the logic that led to the player's waywardness is not uncommon. It is easy for players to get off track and allow their priorities to become skewed. Coaches can help minimize this by reinforcing the relativity of the terms "rich" and "poor." Some people possess tremendous financial means, yet are lonely or lacking true love or suffering from a debilitating illness. They would give up their entire fortune for a clean bill of health. On the other side, some people lack financial wealth but seem to always be happy, healthy, and enjoying life to the fullest. What is rich? What is poor? It is relative.

Players who struggle to grasp this are incapable of becoming good teammates because they always compare themselves to other players on the team. They find it difficult to ever rejoice in the accomplishments of their teammates. Justice can level the playing field and limit this jealousy.

In Chapter 6, I wrote about the quality of service at Disney World. The park is able to sustain that level of service because they watch for combustion statements that lead to combustion points within their processes. Some combustion statements are "This is taking too long" or "No one knows the answer." These are the sort of things guests inevitably say when they start to get frustrated. They indicate that the quality of service cycle is breaking down. Disney management trains its cast members to be attuned to this concept. They want to deal with combustion points before they become explosion points.[60]

I also mentioned earlier in the book how much I dislike the process of cutting players because it is a situation laced with potential volatility. We have been able to apply justice to the process, however, to keep this possible combustion point from becoming an explosion point. When I meet with the team in the preseason, I ask each player to write down how he would like to be cut should he ever find himself in that situation.

It has been my experience that there are benefits to asking them this delicate question up front. First, it makes them aware of their "mortality" as a player. Second, it eases the brunt of the impact of this unpleasant event. We show them respect by honoring their wishes for how they would like to be treated. This is a strategy that any organization can use. When new employees are hired, have them provide an answer to how they would like to be let go (should it ever happen) while they are filling out their initial human resources paperwork.

This simple gesture is a form of justice. By giving the player a say in how the process goes, we remove a large part of the emotional component from the equation. The values of mercy and justice are often intertwined. Conveying grim news or administering punishment in an objective and dispassionate way is merciful justice. Doing this preserves a coach's ability to remain connected to the players without diminishing his capacity to maintain order and build good teammates.

Coaches travel a slippery slope when they make themselves part of the consequences. Players will inescapably make bad decisions that the coach has to deal with. There will be mistakes made on and off the court. If the coach criticizes or ridicules the player too harshly or uses too negative of a tone, he makes himself a part of the consequences, which may turn out to be worse than the actual consequences of the mistake.

The coach's reaction causes the player to dwell on how that makes him feel as opposed to focusing on correcting the error. The coach's reaction is a distraction, and the player becomes resentful. Trust is broken, and self-esteem is damaged.

I once had the misfortune of receiving a speeding ticket. The policeman was professional. He didn't react with emotion. He told me what I did wrong, and gave me the ticket. He didn't belittle me by pointing out how stupid I was for driving too fast, or how inconvenient it was for his day to be interrupted by an idiot like me. After he handed me the ticket, he respectfully told me to have a nice day and went on his way. He let the natural consequences of breaking the law be the punishment. When he drove off, I wasn't cursing him; I was watching my speedometer and obeying the speed limit.

Being hard on a player and verbally jumping on him with the intention of bringing an immediate stop to whatever he was doing wrong may lead to greater competitiveness, and possibly produce more wins, but that's not all it's about. It is also about getting players to learn to be good teammates. Berating players won't contribute to their understanding of how to be good teammates; they will be too emotionally distracted to think about that. It is possible to be demanding without being demeaning. When I was younger, older players would advise me after I got yelled at by the coach that I should hear *what* the coach says, not *how* he says it. Well, how the coach says it does matter. Administering justice in an aggressive and confrontational manner will cause players to think of *their* needs and not the needs of their team.

The flip side of this problem is that if coaches constantly give in to the players and do not hold them accountable, then the coaches are not practicing justice. They are not setting players up to be good teammates. When working toward a common goal, teammates will encounter adversity. Facing that adversity with dignity and poise is an invaluable skill that coaches can teach players through their example.

Another element of justice to consider is the idea of behaving morally and practicing fairness. Obviously, those are two things that any coach would expect good teammates to embody. But the mixture of diverse people can complicate the matter for a team. To be fair, teammates must be empathetic and appreciate the various challenges other players on the team may face.

Sports are frequently referred to as the great equalizer because they have been able to transcend racial and cultural differences. In many ways, how well diversity and tolerance are handled by players in the locker room or clubhouse is a testament to the accuracy of this belief. It is something that I have personally witnessed. The danger for coaches and players, though, is to fall into the trap of thinking that the same kind of equality and acceptance—justice—exists for everyone on the team when they are away from the team setting.

On occasion, I will get a question from the parents of an African-American recruit about the racial make-up of our team. It is a reasonable question as our college is located in an area where there is not a lot of racial diversity. They want their son to be treated fairly, and they are expressing their concern. I used to try to reassure those families that everybody on the team gets a fair chance by telling them, "I don't see color." I stopped using that phrase, however.

Sister Eric Marie got me to see that my response, though well-intentioned, was insensitive. It wasn't an acceptable conveyance of justice. My answer was like trying to put a positive spin on the notorious scene from the Stanley Kubrick film *Full Metal Jacket* in which Gunnery Sergeant Hartman tells his new Marine recruits, "There is no racial bigotry here," then proceeds to rattle off several racial slurs, before adding, "Here you are all equally worthless."[61] I didn't deliver the message with that same blunt tone, but I might as well have.

It is easy to say you only care about how a player produces on the court. Skin color does not matter. Again, that may emphasize the significance of players being competitive, but it won't necessarily turn them into good teammates. A good coach sees color.

What I needed to convey to those families was that not only would their son be treated fairly, but that I was also cognizant of the special challenges minorities face. They needed to be reassured that their son was going to be seen as a unique individual and valued as such.

Because of the unusual makeup of sports teams, minorities in sports can mean something entirely different than what it means to the rest of the world. Take professional sports for example, the most recent racial and gender report acknowledged 68.7% of NFL rosters as being comprised of African-American players.[62] In the NBA, 76.7% of the league's players were identified as persons of color last season, which was down nearly 4% from the previous year.[63] Similar levels of disparity can be seen on sports teams throughout America. The minority is not always a minority.

To compound the matter, there also exists numerous subcultures and sub-groups within teams with their basis rooted in physical size, geographic origins, the position they play, and other things of that nature. In basketball, height is a factor. Tall people have their own unique obstacles. Being tall on the court can be an advantage, but off the court, not so much. When I roomed with seven-foot-five-inch Alan Banister, I got a lesson in the difficulties he faced. "Big Al" had an enormous king-sized bed, but I am not sure he ever got a comfortable night's sleep in even that size of a bed. The heights of chairs, couches, and toilets were less than ideal for him.

Challenges also exist for international players. Challenges exist for players who come from rural areas. Challenges exist for players who come from urban areas. The challenges are everywhere, and coaches have to be aware of all of them.

Now when I am confronted with the question of the racial make-up of our team, I reply, "I don't judge people by the color of their skin, I judge them by the size of their heart." For me, the color of their skin represents all of the various challenges faced by each individual player. I am aware of those challenges, but what matters to me more is their capacity to care for others—the size of their heart.

All kinds of problems can manifest whenever this perspective is missing. As parents, this is something my wife and I have tried to instill in our children. As a coach, it is a concept that I have tried to get our players to adopt. Good teammates have this mentality, and I feel it is important to recognize instances where players put it into practice.

I also feel it is important to recognize when players take the idea a step further and stand up to injustice. This is another way of looking at the value of justice and an intolerance for diversity is certainly an injustice.

All of our players are given a binder at the start of the season. At the beginning of my coaching career, the binders were our play-books. Over the years, they have evolved into much more. Today, the binders are filled with inspirational material that I feel can influence the players' lives for years to come. The binders have grown into a sort of how-to guide for becoming a good teammate.

We begin practice each day with what we call The Page of the Day where I spend a few minutes discussing one page out of the binders with the players. This activity has included such things as John Wooden quotes, Nelson Mandela's inauguration speech, and Robert Frost's poem "The Road Not Taken." Sometimes, Sister Eric Marie will contribute to The Page of the Day by leaving in my campus mailbox a highlighted passage from a book or maga-zine article she has come across. Every now and then, the passage will even be from *ESPN the Magazine*. (Yes, comical as it may be, *that* nun likes sports so much that she has a subscription to *ESPN the Magazine*.)

Players don't always understand our primary objective of teach-ing them to be good teammates, but they understand that playing basketball is fun. I try to leverage their desire to play ball and have fun by making them indulge me for a few minutes of life lessons—The Page of the Day. A favorite page of mine to discuss with the players is the Martin Niemoller's anti-Nazi poem "First They Came."

> *First they came for the Socialists, and I did not speak out—*
> *Because I was not a Socialist.*
> *Then they came for the Trade Unionists, and I did not speak out—*
> *Because I was not a Trade Unionist.*
> *Then they came for the Jews, and I did not speak out—*
> *Because I was not a Jew.*
> *Then they came for me—and there was no one left to speak for me.*[64]

I like presenting this poem to the team because it gives me an opportunity to talk to them about the importance of standing up to injustice and the perils of being complicit by way of neutrality and silence. At the bottom of that binder page, I added in large, bold font the text, "Teammates stand up for those who can't stand up for themselves."

Most players aren't mature enough at this stage of their life to grasp the full gravity of the poem, so I usually add the timeless story of Pee Wee Reese's famous and controversial display of solidarity when he put his arm around Jackie Robinson—his black Brooklyn Dodgers teammate. Without question, it was one of the greatest public displays of the relationship between justice and being a good teammate.

For those unfamiliar with the story, Robinson, the first black player to break the color barrier in major league baseball, had for months been receiving verbal insults, hate mail, and even death threats from angry fans who felt he didn't belong in the league. During one especially difficult game in Cincinnati in which fans were berating Robinson with racial insults, Pee Wee Reese—the popular Dodger's white All-Star shortstop—left his position during the game and walked over to first base to put his arm around Robinson. As Reese stood there with his arm draped over his teammate's shoulder, he smiled at the crowd. It was a significant gesture of solidarity because Reese was from nearby Kentucky and they were playing the game in front of what was considered his hometown. Several decades later, a statue commemorating the event was unveiled outside of a baseball park in Coney Island, New York.

In the end, justice is cutting others slack and making an effort to see things from their perspective. Sometimes, I am annoyed when a player's cell phone rings when I am speaking to the team and they look to see who is calling. Then I start to think about how I would react if it were my cell phone that rang in that instance.

Their actions are viewed as a distraction that seems rude and inconsiderate. But I wrongfully don't see my actions that way. When I look at my phone, it is because it might be my wife calling to say she's been in an accident or that something tragic happened with one of our daughters that needs my urgent attention. The reality is the player's phone could be ringing for the same reasons. My reaction is not that of a just person. Occasionally, we all need to be reminded that justice means tempering our anger and offering a forbearance for infractions until we know all of the details.

12

USING HOSPITALITY TO BUILD GOOD TEAMMATES

A CLOSE relationship exists between each of the Sisters of Mercy values. Examples used to describe mercy could also easily be used to explain justice. Examples from both of them could just as effortlessly be used to demonstrate hospitality.

Take, for instance, the story of Brooklyn Dodger teammates Pee Wee Reese and Jackie Robinson. I used this as an example of the infusion of justice into the process of building good teammates. When Reese walked over and stood beside Jackie Robinson on that fateful day, he wasn't only sending a message about injustice to the hostile Cincinnati fans that were hurling racial insults, he was also conveying his acceptance of Robinson as a teammate. He was being hospitable and publicly welcoming him into their group.

Another example of this crossover of values is the Disney concept of identifying combustion points before they become explosion points. This example was previously used as a way of applying justice, but it can also be a way of preparing to be hospitable.

This is an embarrassing and frightening memory for me, but the first time we took our daughters to Disney World, we had the misfortune of losing our four-year-old in the park. We were walking through Epcot's World Showcase when a torrential rain storm let loose. In the scramble to seek shelter, my wife and I got separated while hustling into the Mexican pavilion. She thought my daughter was with me. I thought my daughter was with her. There were a lot of guests rushing into the building at the same time, and it was a chaotic scene. As soon as we realized she was missing, we panicked. Fortunately, my daughter did not.

She stuck to her training and sought out the nearest Disney cast member. I should note that we had talked to our children ahead of time about what to do if they got lost. In the spirit of preparedness, I had gone to Petco before we went on our trip and bought our daughters dog tags that had their names and our cell phone numbers engraved on the charm. I was afraid that the stress of being lost might prevent them from remembering their phone number or how to spell their name. My daughter was wearing her dog tag when she got lost. (Incidentally, I am aware of how horrible we must sound as parents to have made our child wear pet jewelry and to have succumbed to the cliché of losing our child in *Mexico!*)

Thankfully, everything worked out. The cast member called my cell phone, and we got our daughter back safely. The ordeal was unpleasant, but it was kept from being much worse due largely to how the Disney cast member initially responded. When my daughter approached the cast member, she told the woman she couldn't find her mommy and daddy. The cast member replied, "Oh, it's okay, honey. We lose parents here all the time."

The cast member's calming and reassuring reply was a genuine act of hospitality. She chose her words wisely and kept a combustion point from becoming an explosion point. Had the cast member responded differently, my daughter could have easily burst into tears and been traumatized, and her parents would have probably done the same.

Being guarded with your words—and choosing the right words—are ways of using hospitality to build good teammates.

At the start of a recent school year, we had an incident in which a few of our players failed to exhibit hospitality toward one of our incoming freshman. The way "move-in" happens on our campus, freshman arrive several days before returning students, and they participate in an orientation program. Our dorms were near capacity, so this freshman had been placed in an apartment-style dorm with three upperclassman teammates who hadn't yet arrived. It wasn't the ideal arrangement, but it was certainly workable.

When the freshman moved into his dorm, he picked out a bedroom that seemed to suit his needs and arranged his belongings. A few days later, the first of the upperclassmen arrived and promptly told the freshmen to get his stuff out of that room and move to the other bedroom. Not wanting to make waves, the freshman complied. Shortly after that, the next upperclassman arrived and told the freshman to do the same thing.

Needless to say, the freshman wasn't feeling very welcomed by this point and the frustration of the ordeal sent him off to the housing director to seek a new rooming assignment. Our season hadn't even started, and we already had an unnecessary conflict to deal with. None of them wanted the coach to know what happened, so nobody said anything about the issue to me. I only found out about it because another player on our team, someone who wasn't involved in the fiasco, called me to let me know what had happened. I wasn't happy. Mainly, I was angry with the returning players' lack of hospitality. That was a terrible way to treat a new teammate.

The change in dormitories turned out to be a better situation for the freshman, but the damage done by the upperclassmen to the relationship still needed to be addressed. The first chance I got, I pulled the guilty players aside. Rather than reaming them out, I stole a chapter from the "Tim Kelly leadership manual" and asked them questions intended to lead them to the right conclusion. "Do you think that was the best way to welcome a newcomer to our campus? Do you remember how scary it was for you when you first came to college?"

They understood they had messed up. While I don't want to offer any excuses for their behavior, it seemed to me that part of the problem was my fault. It was too easy for the upperclassman to be confrontational to this freshman because he was still a relative stranger to them. They wouldn't have talked like that to someone they cared about. And the freshman would not have been as sensitive if he was more familiar with the upperclassmen making what he perceived to be unwelcoming demands. The unfamiliarity between players was my fault because I had not provided them with an opportunity to familiarize themselves with each other.

Not long after the dormitory incident, I had everyone on the team—newcomers and veterans alike—participate in an activity that I learned from my daughter's elementary school teacher. Before the start of school, the teacher sent a plain white paper bag to every child in the class with instructions to decorate the outside of the bag in a manner that was representative of their personality. They were then supposed to place four items in the bag that told the story of who they were. My daughter's four items were a photo of her and her sister, an unpopped bag of microwave popcorn, a pink marker, and a flower.

On the first day of school, the students had to present their bag and explain its contents to the class. My daughter said the photo was included because her sister was her "BFF." The popcorn was her favorite afterschool snack. The pink marker was her favorite color, and she likes to draw. The flower represented how much she enjoys playing outside and smelling flowers.

I don't know where the teacher got the idea, but I liked it. The limit of having only four things in the bag forced my daughter to showcase only the main bullet points of her life. It was insightful to see what she prioritized and how she saw herself. It was just as interesting when I had our players do the white paper bag exercise with their fellow teammates.

Some of the players' choices were very predicable—photos of their girlfriends, logos from their favorite sports teams, and images of musicians or athletes whom they admired. Some of their choices, though, were quite revealing. One player included a dollar bill because his favorite uncle had given him advice when he was younger that he should always keep a dollar in his pocket for a rainy day. Another player put measuring spoons in his bag, explaining that he liked to cook. Perhaps the most moving inclusion was the dog tags of a player's deceased older brother.

The exercise was a healthy and creative way of getting the players to open up about themselves. I felt I was accelerating their teammate care curve with this activity. In fact, the bags were so well received that I decided to do my own bag and share its contents with the players. After all, they deserved to gain some insight into the person coaching them. On top of that, my participation was also a way of showing that I trusted them by sharing my personal life.

In case you are wondering, my bag included a photo of my family, a jar of my favorite barbecue sauce, a photo of my Hard Rock Café t-shirt collection, and a silver whistle engraved with the phrase, "#1 Dad" that my daughters had given me for Father's Day. (My girls told me the whistle was to remind me to come home when I was done coaching for the day.)

The white paper bag activity is now a mainstay of our basketball program. It is good for the new players to learn a little bit about the players already on the team. It is good for the veteran players to learn a little bit about the new players, too. Of course, it is always good for both of them to learn something about their coach. That is hospitality in action.

Sister Eric Marie is fond of telling a story about Catherine McAuley, the Irish foundress of the Sisters of Mercy, and a woman who had sought refuge at her House of Mercy. Life was not easy for women in Ireland in the 19th century, especially those who were the age of this young lady. Many of them were homeless and, to keep from starving, they often resorted to prostitution.

One night, the young woman knocked on the House of Mercy's door, seeking shelter for the night. The house was already full, and McAuley found herself additionally skeptical of the purity of the woman's motives. She turned the woman away. The next day, McAuley found herself overwhelmed with regret that she had denied shelter to someone who could have been in need of help and was fearful that something bad had happened to the young woman. From that moment on, McAuley declared it is better to be fooled and taken advantage of, than to risk being wrong and allow a tragedy to occur. Sadly, in those days, desperate women who had nowhere else to go often took their lives by drowning themselves.

In many ways, the story captures the basis for the Sisters of Mercy's theory on the importance of hospitality. Coaches sometimes have players on their team whose apparent authenticity causes the coach to be skeptical. The player says and does all of the right things in front of the coach, but as soon as he is outside of earshot, the player shows his true colors. When a coach is burdened by this type of *Eddie Haskell-esque* player, it is probably best to follow McAuley's example of being hospitable and setting skepticism aside.

Another way to show hospitality towards this particular kind of player may be to heed the recommendation of another strong-minded woman—Mary Kay Ash. As the founder of Mary Kay cosmetic products, Ash said, "Pretend that every single person you meet has a sign around his or her neck that says, 'Make me feel important.'"[65] If a coach can get the player to feel important, his phoniness will gradually fade. *Eddie Haskell-esque* players are the types of players that are craving the coach's attention.

The coach feeds their attention-starved ego when he makes them feel important. Sister Eric Marie is exceptionally good at this. She is so kind and generous that players start to feel like they have been placed on a pedestal. They love how good it feels on that pedestal so much that they will make incredible sacrifices not to fall off of it. Coaches can create a pedestal by identifying distinctive roles for players, especially roles that usually don't get a lot of attention.

If a player shows an inclination for cheering when another teammate makes a good play, put extra effort into complimenting his actions. Tell him, "Wow, you give the best high-fives!" Then, turn to the rest of the team and say, "You know you did something good whenever he gives you a high-five. That guy gives the best high-fives!"

Now that player has been placed on a pedestal. He has an identity. It won't matter if he is the best player on the team or the worst. He has something to embrace that is not directly related to the box score. He will go out of his way to live up to that identity and, in doing so, his actions have the potential to impact positively his teammates' performances.

Being hospitable is, to a great extent, about making people feel comfortable. When you focus on the needs of others and try to help them meet those needs, you show how much you care about them, which makes them feel comfortable. Soon, they begin to open up and share with you and eventually even listen to you, all of which are hallmarks of being a good teammate.

People are generally comfortable around those who are humble. Sister Eric Marie will always see herself as a coal miner's daughter. That is one of the main reasons people are so comfortable in her presence. Her perspective puts people at ease, just as it does for others who are humble. On the other hand, people who are arrogant are not hospitable because they make those around them uncomfortable.

Regrettably, in sports, some of the most arrogant people are poor losers. It almost pains me to write that. Not so much that I thought I was arrogant, but because I know what a poor loser I was. I used to subscribe to the Vince Lombardi mentality of, "Show me a good loser, and I'll show you a loser." If we lost a game, my friends and family knew to keep their distance; I was a miserable person to be around. But like a lot of other things, Sister Eric Marie brought about a change in my attitude towards losing.

Our team had just lost in the championship game of a tournament, one which was hosted by our rival. It was an impressive accomplishment for us to have advanced as far as we did. We had pulled off an upset over a team that was much better than us in the previous game. Because of that upset, we were riding high into the championship game and everybody, myself included, felt we were a lock to win it all.

However, we played nowhere near as well in the championship game as we had in the previous game, and we ended up losing by a close margin. I was very disappointed. We tried to make a last-ditch comeback attempt by fouling and putting the other team on the free-throw line in the final seconds. In retrospect, all that strategy really did was stop the clock and give the crowd an opportunity to see our players wallow in self-pity. The game's outcome was already decided by the time we tried to implement our fouling strategy, and it made the situation worse.

The players' body language continued to be incredibly depressing when it came time to accept the runner-up trophy. I got stuck talking to some people right after the awards presentation and the players got to the locker room ahead of me. This is not an entirely uncommon occurrence, so they knew just to sit quietly and wait for me to come in and say a few words before they started changing out of their uniforms. Much to my surprise, however, I could hear someone already speaking to the team as I opened the locker room door.

I thought to myself, who could be so brazen as to challenge the unwritten rule of not talking to the team after the game before I did? Lo and behold, it was Sister Eric Marie. She was already in the locker room dispensing wisdom. Well, what was I going to do—yell at a nun for breaking the taboo? Not a chance.

The door was near the back of the locker room, and no one could see me when I entered. I stood there for a few moments and listened to what Sister Eric Marie said to the players. She was telling them how proud she was of how they played and congratulating them on their effort. That was not exactly what I had intended to relay to them.

She kept talking, and then she began also to scold them for being poor sports. She said they had not played as bad as they were acting, and that the other team just happened to play phenomenally well—something that was beyond their control.

The more I listened, the more I realized she was right. We had not played that terrible. We executed the things we wanted to and exceeded most of our statistical goals. The other team just played better than us.

Sister Eric Marie mentioned to the players that the way they were acting discounted our opponent's efforts, and that it was arrogant and disrespectful. We were not practicing hospitality. In essence, she was telling them that, win or lose, they have to be humble, and humility comes from recognizing one's limitations.

Somewhere in the middle of her talk, it occurred to me that she was also right in that there does not have to be a correlation between your mood and the outcome. Your mood should be a reflection of the satisfaction that comes from knowing you gave your best. If you fall short of these expectations, then your mood should be reflective of your commitment to do better going forward. If a coach is going to commit to building good teammates, then he needs to exemplify that belief himself.

However, be cautious. Humility may come from recognizing your limitations, but you can become so humble that you sell yourself short. Part of being a good teammate is going out, competing, and discovering what you are capable of achieving. You have an obligation to show you care about your teammates by giving your best effort while bearing in mind that doing so does not necessarily guarantee victory. The key, therefore, is not to be a good loser but a gracious loser.

A good loser is arrogant and is not a good teammate. A gracious loser demonstrates hospitality and is a good teammate.

13

USING SERVICE TO BUILD GOOD TEAMMATES

IF there was an eleventh commandment, I believe it would be "Thou shall serve others." In keeping with the theme of this book, it could be more appropriately phrased "Thou shall serve thy teammates."

In the early days of the Sisters of Mercy, the women working under Catherine McAuley were often known as the "walking nuns," due to how visible they were in their communities.[66] The Sisters of Mercy were always out walking the streets of Dublin, serving the needs of the underprivileged. This was unusual because most women of religious orders were bound by the traditional confines of a convent. The uncommon visibility of the sisters was indicative of their vow to serve the needs of others. While the Sisters of Mercy have evolved in many ways since then, their visible commitment to service is just as evident today.

Service is a crucial component of building good teammates because it shows a player's capacity to care about something other than himself. It is a sign of selflessness—a characteristic of someone who can be trusted. The concept of a servant leader is ageless, yet it continues to be a buzzword in modern day leadership discussions. The servant leaders should not be as focused on the application of power as on helping meet the needs of those under their command. A servant leader shares power.

One day, after our team had finished working out, I observed the team's captain unintentionally partake in a non-servant leadership act. The team was doing a strength and conditioning workout with heavy, oversized tires that they had to put back in storage when training ended. I heard the captain say, "Freshmen, get the tires put away." In years past, that would have been business as usual, but we had been emphasizing building good teammates, and his approach was contrary to our new philosophy.

Later that day, I talked to the player about what I had witnessed. He was a great kid, but his immediate response was, "I'm sorry, Coach. I didn't mean it like that. I will just put the tires away myself next time."

Although I admired his willingness to humble himself and do the job, he had missed my point. As the season progressed, the captain was going to acquire more and more responsibilities. If he carried on solving the problem by doing it himself, his teammates would grow to feel very entitled. They would always expect him to take care of whatever was needed. It would only be a matter of time before he stretched himself too thin, and the burden of serving in that manner would turn him into a bad teammate.

Servant leadership isn't about the leader doing everything himself. It is about the leader finding a way to help those around him see the value that comes from investing in the process. What the captain should have done is say to the freshmen players, "Hey, can you give me a hand putting these away?" Then he should have accompanied them and at least partially assisted in the endeavor.

That would have sent the message to the younger players that whatever job they were asked to do—in this case, put the tires away—must be important because the captain was participating. It would have also prevented resentment or entitlement. Eventually, the other players would come to appreciate the significance of these seemingly menial tasks and take the initiative without being asked. The captain would no longer need to get involved. As players climb the ranks, that mentality will endure.

When a leader wants to move teammates away from compliance and toward commitment, it is usually better to appeal to

161

their sense of pride and give them a reputation to live up to, rather than force them into submission through guilt. This was the advice Warren Buffett gave to U2 frontman Bono when the rock star sought the billionaire's counsel on how to inspire Americans to join in the battle to end poverty in Africa. Buffett said: "Don't appeal to the conscience of America. Appeal to the greatness of America and you'll get the job done."[67]

In other words, Bono would fail if he were to guilt Americans into helping his cause. "How can the citizens of the wealthiest nation in the world stand by idly and not care about this problem?" Instead, he needed to stroke their ego to inspire them. "You're the greatest country in the world, if anybody can help solve this problem, it is you." Guilting teammates into service is compliance. Inspiring teammates to serve is reinforcing commitment.

Great leaders are able to do this, mainly because they are obsessed with the well-being of those they serve. Another great philanthropist, Milton S. Hershey, exemplified this as well as anyone.

My wife loves chocolate. And for this reason, we have on occasion, visited Hershey, Pennsylvania, the headquarters of the Hershey Company. Appropriately nicknamed "The Sweetest Place on Earth," the town is a chocoholic's paradise. During one of our visits, we stayed at the famous Hershey Hotel. The history of this magnificent building is a marvel in and of itself.

During the Great Depression, Milton S. Hershey made a decision to use his money to create jobs and keep his town from suffering the economic hardships seen by the rest of America. Most of those jobs were related to the numerous building projects the company had purposely undertaken. The luxury hotel was one of those projects. During its construction, a foreman brought Hershey to the site to show him a new mechanical wonder known as a steam shovel. The foreman told him it was able to do the work of 40 men. Hershey promptly replied with instructions for the foreman to get rid of it and hire 40 men.[68] That story always struck me as epitomizing how much care a coach should have for his players.

Surely it would have been more economical and more efficient for the company to have made use of the steam shovel. However, that would have been counter to Hershey's primary objective of serving the needs of his people. His intention was to create jobs and thwart the effects of the Depression on his town. He was not aiming to save the company money.

If Hershey's company were to go bankrupt, though, his efforts could have become a moot point. However, there was a low probability of that happening. The financial losses he would bear were worthwhile in his estimation. Any potential financial gain the company would have received from using the more-efficient steam shovel was so minimal that it didn't even factor into his decision.

When it comes to building good teammates, one of my more controversial beliefs involves the distribution of playing time. Although it may be in line with how Hershey viewed the steam shovel, it is a polarizing philosophy and contrary to the conventional approach to coaching.

An essential element in getting players to become good teammates is giving them a chance to play during the games. I understand how this can be seen as counter to the competitive mentality of playing the game with the intention of winning. Reducing the playing time of the team's best players could result in a loss. But the point is, at the amateur level, the primary objective should be to build good teammates, not win games. This is comparable to Hershey's main goal of creating jobs, not improving his company's financial statement.

As coaches, we continually stress to players the importance of serving the team, yet we don't always give everyone on the team the opportunity to help in the most obvious way—contributing in the games. In the past, I did my best to convince all of the players on the team that they were important. I often used the analogy that a team is like an iceberg. Only the top 10% of the iceberg is seen above water, but it's the other 90% that causes the damage. I would remind them that it was the 90% that floated below the waterline that sank the Titanic, and that the players on the bench were like the unseen bottom portion of the iceberg.

I believe that every player on the team is important. However, I have come to acknowledge that my message is viewed with little

163

more than lip service from the players' perspective. They want to play. That is the main reason they are there. When they don't get to play, there is little that can be said that will offset their dissatisfaction.

A coach can try to encourage them to keep working hard. Sometimes, such as a situation where a player is playing behind an older, more experienced teammate, the coach can temporarily stave off the dissatisfaction by reminding him that his time will come. You couldn't do that, though, if an older player were playing behind a younger, more talented player. The reality is that practically the only remaining way for bench players to get meaningful playing time is for something bad to happen to the teammate playing ahead of them—an injury, a subpar performance, etc.

When a player is left with no other option for getting playing time than to depend on the misfortune of his fellow teammate, it is not going to foster an environment where the emphasis is building good teammates. Even if done subconsciously, rooting against a teammate is not healthy for the team. Inevitably, the dysfunction caused by this will tear the team apart.

It is a complex problem because players also want the team to win. Coaches might have an ulterior agenda in coaching with the purpose of building good teammates, instead of the goal of winning games. Players, however, may not fully appreciate the depth of the coach's agenda. Failure to recognize this issue could result in rendering the coach's primary objective irrelevant, similar to Hershey's primary objective becoming moot if his company went bankrupt.

This raises difficult questions. How many players can be on a team's roster before the possibility of everyone getting playing time becomes farfetched? How many players can a coach play in a game without putting the team at a competitive disadvantage? There are a lot of variables that factor into those questions, and I don't know the exact answer. I do know that the number of players is a lot higher than most coaches accept as the limit.

At Grinnell College in Iowa, their men's NCAA Division III basketball team has for years been playing considerably more players in a game than most teams do. Grinnell typically has over 20 players on their roster. Rarely do they ever play fewer than 15 players in a single game. In fact, it is routine for them to play as many as 18 or 19 players in a game. That is profound when you figure that there can only be 5 players on the court at a time and that most teams play only 7 or 8 kids in a game.

The reason Grinnell is able to do this is because of their up-tempo style of play. They push the ball up the court on offense and apply nonstop full-court pressure on the defense. The fatigue factor that is brought on by this pace necessitates multiple players getting court time. Grinnell is an excellent example of a team who has adapted their style of play to accommodate greater participation. They are also proof that a team can get a lot of players into the game while still being competitive.

There are plenty of examples of other basketball teams that use high levels of in-game participation. There are plenty of examples of teams from other sports that successfully do so as well. If a coach is going to legitimately serve the team, then he or she must give the players a chance to help the team by finding them playing time. Teams that have elevated levels of participation tend to produce better teammates in the long run, regardless of their overall win/loss record.

It is ironic because the players on those teams could conceivably develop a sense of entitlement by always getting into games. They know they are going to get to play no matter what they do. It doesn't, however, work that way.

Players on those teams gain the experience of realizing that the performance of every teammate factors into the success of the team. In the corporate world, an organization's success is not solely dependent on the performance of its top few salesmen. They may have a big impact on it, but it's not the only thing that has an impact. The proficiency of the receptionists, the mailroom clerks, and the maintenance staff also plays a role in that success. They are all dependent upon each other.

When I was in eighth grade, I had the opportunity to play on a team where the league mandated that everyone on the roster got playing time. Like most teams, we had a noticeable talent gap between our top players and our "bench" players. There was one player that was especially lacking the physical skills to play the game. He was big and slow for his age and he struggled to run as fast as the other kids. He also did not have the finesse or experience to be a proficient dribbler, shooter, or passer. Clearly, this hampered the extent to which he was capable of contributing.

We were all friends with this player, and we accepted that he had to play in the games. We knew it wasn't the coach's decision but a league rule. When he was put into the game, we didn't resent it. We realized it was in our best interest to encourage him from the sidelines and to be appreciative of any contribution he was able to make. Our encouragement had to prompt his best efforts, too. That experience left a mark on me.

Incidentally, that player grew up to become a manager at a large grocery store, where he was directly responsible for overseeing the checkout process and the performance of all of the cashiers. Many of them were inexperienced teenagers or individuals who otherwise did not possess the most polished social skills. They all seemed to love and respect him, though. Sometimes I would go into the store and watch him interact with his employees. It was inspiring to see how kind he was to them and how appreciative they were of him. I have to believe that his experience of playing on our team and how he was treated played a part in how he treated those workers.

If I could wave a magic wand and change one thing about organized amateur sports, it would be for all governing bodies to adopt mandatory participation rules. With those rules, it would take the burden off the coach of trying to convince the players of the value of everyone on the team getting to play in the games. Parents, players, and fans would come to accept the rule. Perhaps it would test the creativity of coaches with how they could successfully work every player into the game, but it would level the competitive playing field if all teams were required to do it. Surely, rules like this would be tremendously beneficial in helping coaches in their quest to build good teammates.

Previously, I mentioned our tradition of getting our team together at the start of each season to watch the movie *Hoosiers*. There are so many good lessons to be learned from this film. One scene that I frequently use as an example of subtle yet effective service to a teammate is when the smaller, less talented Ollie is put on the free-throw line with a chance to win the game.

As the teams come out of a timeout, a bigger, stronger player from the opposition deliberately bumps into Ollie and tries to intimidate him by saying, "I didn't know they grew 'em so small down on the farm."

What happens next is as good an example as I can imagine of a teammate providing service. Ollie's more confident teammate, Merle, gives him a pat on the back and discreetly tells him, "Hey, don't worry about that. You just concentrate on what you're doing and put it in the hole, right? You can do it."[69]

There was no *rah! rah!* speech. No get-in-your-face moment. No calling his teammate out. Just a few subtle words of encouragement that injected an incredible amount of confidence into young Ollie. That's genuine servant leadership. It does not always have to be loud, blunt candor. Sometimes the best messages are delivered quietly and privately. These are commonly the types of messages that bear the most fruitful results and build the greatest loyalty.

I try to reinforce the notion that even small contributions can impact the game, even if the small contribution is getting into the game and not making a mistake. Sometimes the absence of an error is a positive contribution. I used to try to fire up our players when they gathered together for our last huddle before the game tipped off. I don't do that anymore. Now I get them together, maybe offer a last minute reminder or two about the game plan, and then have them all recite—in unison—a short poem they have memorized. It is a variation of an Edward Everett Hale quote that goes like this:

I am only one.
But I am one.
I can't do everything.
But I can do something.
What I can do, I ought to do.
What I ought to do, I shall do.

I think it reminds them that every contribution matters, and it gets them to search for something they can do to help the team. They feel obliged to come up with something, and they feel committed to putting whatever they come up with to use. I think it also makes them acutely aware of each member of the team's limitations, including their own, and each member of the team's unique gifts. This allows players to serve in different ways.

Somewhere in the course of this realization, they learn that every now and then service to the team means simply stepping outside of their comfort zone.

A while back, I asked Sister Eric Marie to help promote our team and participate in a video that would be played during our version of Midnight Madness. The video was a parody of an old McDonald's commercial featuring Michael Jordan and Larry Bird in which they play a game of HORSE for a Big Mac. In our video, Sister Eric Marie happens upon several of our basketball players moping around the gym. She convinces them that the best way to relieve their stress is to get up and start playing, and then she challenges them to a game of PIG. (Our video had time constraints and couldn't accommodate a game of HORSE.) Just like the McDonald's commercial, and to the surprise of our players, she starts shooting crazy shots with her eyes shut that go over the rafters and end with "nothing but net."

The video was hugely popular. In fact, we put it on YouTube and it has received several thousand hits and has been seen by viewers all over the world. Sister Eric Marie had to step out of her comfort zone a bit to do the video, but she saw it as a way for her to serve the needs of our students. To her, giving hugs to wayward souls and stepping out of her comfort zone to film a funny video are both done in the spirit of service to others. There is a degree of sacrifice involved with both of those undertakings that reinforces the idea that service can come in a variety of ways—and all of them matter.

Here is a final word on service and its relationship to building good teammates. It is widely accepted that people gain happiness through service to others. Making others happy makes *you* feel happy. It can get to a point where people become so addicted to helping others that they seek opportunities to do so, just to make themselves feel good. Their gratification becomes their motive. This may be the one time where coaches should tolerate their players being selfish. If using their talents to provide service to others leads to increased self-satisfaction, then players should, by all means, be encouraged to serve. It will undoubtedly lead to them becoming better teammates and to the team excelling at an exponential rate.

14

WHY IT ALL MATTERS— HER LAST WORDS

MY mother-in-law is an avid reader. She has an odd practice, though, of flipping to the end of a book and reading the last chapter first. I have given her considerable grief over the years about doing this, and I chuckle at her insistence of continuing to do so in spite of my jeering. She defends her actions by explaining that she likes to know how a book ends before she starts reading it.

I may not agree with her strange logic, but I do understand it. To really appreciate the beginning of a story, it helps to know how it ends. And vice versa.

For me, more important than the beginning or the ending of a story, however, is what transpires in between. It's a lot like Linda Ellis's brilliant poem *The Dash* that describes the significance of the punctuation mark that lies between the two dates inscribed on a tombstone. It is what a person did between the date they were born and the date they died that matters.[70] In large part, this book was written with the intention of adding something of genuine substance to *my* dash.

I make no pretense of being an unusually gifted writer, nor of having all the answers. I am just a guy who decided to stop being part of the problem and start trying to be part of the solution. I'm a coach who arrived at the conclusion that he was doing it the wrong way. Teaching players to be competitive is good, but teaching them to be good teammates is better. Good teammates will always be in demand, and coaching them this way will prepare them for a successful life long after they are finished with sports.

Writing this book was my attempt to heed my own advice to be a good teammate. I *cared* about a problem. I tried to *share* what I had learned and what I thought could be done to correct it. And I *listened* to my heart telling me to step outside of my comfort zone and put pen to paper. Now, I am hoping that others will also listen and will come to care about the problem as much as I do.

There were times when I got frustrated and came close to abandoning this project. In those moments, Sister Eric Marie would remind me of things that Catherine McAuley, founder of the Sisters of Mercy, had to say about perseverance. A favorite of mine came from a letter McAuley wrote to Sister Mary Anne Doyle, the first young woman to offer her services to the Dublin House of Mercy. "Do not fear offending anyone. Speak as your mind directs and always act with...courage..."[71]

My wife, ever the Disney enthusiast, took a slightly different approach. She quoted lines from Disney movies to me. My favorite from her came via Dory in *Finding Nemo*. "Just keep swimming. Just keep swimming."[72]

Everyone has their version of a personal Mount Rushmore—the four individuals who had the biggest influence on their life. I am eternally grateful for the things I learned from all of the men on my Mount Rushmore—even my father. Sometimes, learning is discovering how to do things. Sometimes, learning is discovering how *not* to do things. Both of those are accurate when it comes to the example my father set. There were times when his choices hurt me, and it resulted in us having a very tumultuous, and ultimately estranged relationship.

For those reasons, I thought about finding someone else to write about. But after further consideration, I decided none of the men on my Mount Rushmore were perfect. They were human, and they also had their faults. But that is the great thing about history. We can choose to dust away the bad parts and focus on the good.

In the end, it is better to adhere to the paraphrased translation of a Buddhist belief that holding on to anger is like grasping a hot coal with the intent of throwing it at someone else—you are the one who gets burned.

This is a concept that good teammates understand better than anybody. If you are around a group long enough—like a team—you are bound to fall victim to familiarity breeding contempt. Friction is inevitable and so is anger. When teammates handle these situations with mercy, it shows they care.

Players who truly care can be trusted because their motives are pure. They have no hidden agendas. They will always have the team's best interests at heart.

While I was discussing my ideas for this book with a friend, he raised an interesting question. How can you tell how much a teammate really cares? We brainstormed for answers for a long while, trying to identify what visible cues we could use to calculate the extent of a player's care. In the course of our discussion, I found an intriguing article from the *New York Times* about a study done by a group of researchers at Cal-Berkley on tactile communication in the NBA. They counted all of the high-fives, fist bumps, pats on the back, and hugs that happened during an entire NBA season and concluded that the most successful teams had the highest number of "touches."[73]

Maybe there is a correlation between physical contact and success on the court. A teammate who cares about other teammates would certainly be inclined to extend physical expressions of his emotions. In the study, they determined the Boston Celtics and the Los Angeles Lakers—the teams that won the NBA championships the year before the study and the year of the study, respectively—to be the league's most "touch-bonded" teams.[74] Of course, those teams could have just been more talented or lucky and had more reasons to give high-fives.

We considered that, and eventually, my friend and I agreed that success on the court does not necessarily guarantee players are being taught to be good teammates. Quantifying care falls under the guidelines of the adage, "Not everything that can be counted counts, and not everything that counts can be counted." Identifying teammates who care is primarily the result of a gut feeling, and that is why coaching is still more of an art than a science.

Finding ways to detect care requires creativity, resourcefulness, and an always-observant eye. The same could be said for identifying teammates who share. It is exponentially easier to see the obvious examples of players who share, but sometimes the subtler instances have the biggest impact, such as players who share their time or knowledge with a teammate even though that sharing has the potential to negatively affect their playing time or the amount of publicity they may receive. Teammates who share can not only be trusted but are also capable of trusting others.

A few months ago, I walked into my office and found that Sister Eric Marie had left a gift on my desk.

She is a huge proponent of educating men to be good fathers, specifically fathers who have daughters. When girls grow up, the quality of their relationship with their father will be the standard to which they hold their future boyfriends and husbands. Girls who had a positive relationship with their father will be far more prone to seek healthier, romantic relationships and they will not settle for poor treatment. Sister Eric Marie believes that educating men to be good fathers is at the heart of decreasing the problem of domestic and sexual violence against women. She apparently is not the only one to think this way.

The NFL Players Association partnered with A Call to Men—a national violence prevention organization—and put out a book with inspiring stories of NFL personalities and their relationships with their daughters. On the cover of *NFL Dads Dedicated to Daughters: Inspiring Personal Accounts on Fatherhood from the Men of the NFL* there is a picture of Hall of Fame running back Jerome Bettis and his daughter.[75] This book was the gift Sister Eric Marie left on my desk.

Given the recent discussions she and I had been having about this issue, I thought the book was a thoughtful gesture on her part. However, when I opened the book, I found a hand-written note from Jerome Bettis to me on the inside cover and realized Sister Eric Marie's gift wasn't just thoughtful, it was pretty cool! I wondered how she came to get him to write in the book, and the story goes something like this...

Jerome Bettis is a spokesperson for S&T Bank, which was running a promotion in which each of its branch offices was asked to send a customer representative to a luncheon where the former Pittsburgh Steeler would be the guest speaker. Sister Eric Marie is a loyal S&T Bank patron, and she was chosen to be her branch's representative. (What can I say, I am not the only one who loves *that* nun.) After the luncheon, Sister Eric Marie and a few of the other guests were invited to attend a private social with Bettis, who evidently fell victim to her charm just like everyone else who comes into contact with her. The rest of the story is, as they say, history.

By birthright, I grew up a Pittsburgh Steelers fan. Everyone from western Pennsylvania is automatically indoctrinated into the Steelers nation. I had never met Bettis, so I asked Sister Eric Marie what she thought of him. She said, "Oh, he is a nice guy." I had to laugh because I know what a negative stigma often accompanies that phrase in the sports world, as in, nice guys finish last.

Too frequently, good teammates are perceived as nice guys and have to battle the negative vibe associated with that label. I believe, however, that the person who said nice guys finish last was too impatient and didn't take a large enough sample. In the end, nice guys are the only ones who finish.

I appreciated Sister Eric Marie's willingness to share with me the NFL book and her experience of obtaining it. But then again, that's what good teammates do—they share. I also appreciated Sister Eric Marie's patience and willingness to listen to all of my questions while collecting information for this project, reaffirming the conviction that good teammates listen.

Coaches who emphasize competitiveness are grateful to players who listen to their instructions. It gives the game plan a chance to work and keeps everybody on the team on the same page. Coaches who emphasize building good teammates are additionally grateful to players who listen to their fellow teammates. This keeps teammates in touch with how the other players on the team are thinking and feeling. Listening to them is a way to reciprocate trust and convey empathy.

There is a likeability factor to good teammates, especially those who listen. Others want to be around them and serve their needs because others know that good teammates are well-versed in service *and* mercy *and* justice *and* hospitality. Good teammates epitomize these values, and that's what makes them nice people. In this regard, we should all listen to the advice of Angelo Dundee, the longtime boxing trainer of Muhammad Ali, when he said, "Be nice, it don't cost nothing."[76]

If we, as a society, don't change the way we are coaching amateur sports, the value of sports participation will go by the wayside. Times have changed. There are simply too many other extracurricular activities competing for kids' attention these days. When you factor in the economic strain on our schools, it is inevitable that school-sponsored sports will face elimination. School officials won't be able to justify funding sports, and it will be hard to argue against their point. What sustainable value will funding sports bring to the table?

However, if we can make a better effort to emphasize coaching kids to be good teammates, we can prevent amateur sports from becoming obsolete. After all, good teammates will always be in demand. No one can dispute that fact. Building good teammates will keep sports relevant and funding the effort to do so will forever be a worthwhile investment for society.

When my daughters were toddlers, I loved coming home and holding them in my arms. Those were, and still are, some of the best moments of my life. Somehow, I seemed always to be wearing polo shirts embroidered with the Nike swoosh symbol and the Mount Aloysius College (MAC) logo during those moments. Because of that, the first words my oldest daughter ever spoke were—in this order—Dad, Nike, and Mac.

Many years from now, I hope the last words she ever speaks are, "Be good teammates." In the spirit of paying it forward, I hope they are spoken to people willing to continue emphasizing the idea of teaching kids to be good teammates above all else.

Good teammates care. Good teammates share. Good teammates listen. Be a good teammate.

ENDNOTES

Chapter 1

1 National Association of Basketball Coaches, College Basketball Student-Athletes of All Levels. 2014. Print. (*Information about the Allstate NABC Good Works Team was gathered from a press release sent by Rick Leddy, Senior Director of Communication for the NABC.)

2 www.city-data.com/city/Johnsonburg-Pennsylvania.html

3 Marx, Jeffrey. "He Turns Boys Into Men." *Parade* August 29, 2004: 4-6.

4 Marx, Jeffrey. *Season of Life*. New York: Simon & Schuster, 2003.

5 www.ncaa.org/about/resources/research/ncaa-social-environments-study

6 "Millennials in Adulthood: Detached from Institutions, Networked with Friends." Pew Research Center. www.pewsocialtrends.org/2014/03/07/millennials-in-adulthood/ (March 7, 2014).

7 www.ncaa.org/about/resources/research/probability-competing-beyond-high-school

8 www.instagram.com/p/6aXCJ2JFi5/?taken-by=jhharrison92 (August 15, 2015).

Chapter 2

9 www.jaha.org/FloodMuseum/RedCross.html

10 *Slapshot*. Directed by George Roy Hill. 1977. Universal Pictures.

11 www.simon.com/Mall/LeasingSheet/7704_KingOfPrussia_SCO2033MasterOverview.pdf

12 "Americans and Social Trust: Who, Where and Why." Pew Research Center. www.pewsocialtrends.org/2007/02/22/americans-and-social-trust-who-where-and-why/ (February 22, 2007).

13 www.lincolnhighway.jameslin.name/history/part1.html

14 The S.S. Grand View Point Hotel. www.lhhc.org/shiphotel.asp

15 www.cr.nps.gov/nr/research/

16 "Wooden's Wisdom." Vol. II. no. 122. (March 11, 2014).

17 Lipman, Victor. "New Employee Study Shows Recognition Matters More Than Money." Psychology Today. www.psychologytoday.com/blog/mind-the-manager/201306/new-employee-study-shows-recognition-matters-more-money (June 13, 2003).

Chapter 3

18 "Building Trust." Ken Blanchard Companies. www.kenblanchard.com/img/pub/Blanchard-Building-Trust.pdf (n.d.).

19 "Building Trust." Ken Blanchard Companies. www.kenblanchard.com/img/pub/Blanchard-Building-Trust.pdf, n.d.

20 Walsh, Matt. "The Thailand to Burma Railway." www.amosa.org.au/schools/mhp/ww2/The%20Burma-Thailand%20(Death)%20Railway.pdf (2005).

21 *Bridge on the River Kwai*. Directed by David Lean. 1957. Columbia Pictures.

22 Rowley, Tom. "Burma Railway: British POW breaks silence over horrors." www.telegraph.co.uk/history/world-war-two/10382906/Burma-Railway-British-POW-breaks-silence-over-horrors.html (October 18, 2013).

23 www.campgreylock.com/about.php

24 Bradley, Robert, Guido Guida, and John Grasso. "The History of Olympic Basketball." www.apbr.org/olympics.html (n.d.).

25 Osburn, Chris. "Potcheen: Ireland's Moonshine." Drinking Made Easy. www.drinkingmadeeasy.com/blog/potcheen-irelands-moonshine/ (May 2011).

Chapter 4

26 Hearing, Stephen D. *Refeeding Syndrome Is Underdiagnosed and Undertreated, but Treatable*. www.ncbi.nlm.nih.gov/pmc/articles/PMC390152/ (April 17, 2004).

27 For more information on Eric Kapitulik and *The Program*: www.theprogram.org.

Chapter 5

28 Jimenez, Tony. "Garrett getting the most among programs with so little." *Basketball Times*, November 2009: 64.

29 www.garrettcountyweather.com/garrett-annual-snowfall/

30 www.deepcreektimes.com/snowfall.asp

31 www.weather.com/news/weather-winter/20-snowiest-large-cities-america-20140130?pageno=2

32 McNaught-Watson, Barbara. "Maryland Winters: Snow, Wind, Ice and Cold." www.erh.noaa.gov/lwx/winter/md-winter.html (n.d.).

33 Rodricks, Dan. "Chronicling Maryland's 'Sweet Spot for Snow'." The Baltimore Sun. www.articles.baltimoresun.com/2014-02-13/news/bs-md-rodricks-0213-20140213_1_garrett-county-much-snow-first-snow (February 3, 2014).

34 Hochman, Stan. "Grand Cannon Big 5 Hall Of Famer Learned Early That Life Is No Gimme." Philly.com. www.articles.philly.com/1990-02-06/sports/25882752_1_alfa-romeo-public-league-parade-magazine-all-america (February 6, 1990).

35 Dungy, Tony. *The Mentor Leader: Secrets to People and Teams that Win Consistently*. 158. Winter Park, Florida: Tyndale House Publishers, 2010.

Chapter 6

36 Lou Holtz was the Presidential Guest Speaker at the 2011 Annual Meeting of the American Academy of Orthopaedic Surgeons. This quote was said during that speech. For more information: www.aaos.org/news/acadnews/2011/AAOS11_2_18.asp.

37 Jones, Bruce. "A Leadership Lesson: The Role of Positive Peer Pressure in Workplace Culture." Disney Institute. www.disneyinstitute.com/blog/2015/02/a-leadership-lesson-the-role-of-positive-peer-pressure-in-workplace-culture/330/ (February 19, 2015).

38 Barnes, Brooks. "In Customer Service Consulting, Disney's Small World Is Growing." The New York Times. www.nytimes.com/2012/04/22/business/media/in-business-consulting-disneys-small-world-is-growing.html?_r=2 (April 21, 2012).

Chapter 7

None.

Chapter 8

39 www.londonstockexchange.com/about-the-exchange/company-overview/our-history/our-history.htm

40 DeVenzio, Dick. *Stuff Good Players Should Know*. Charlotte: Fool Court Press, 1983.

41 Markman, Art. "How One Simple Change Can Make You A Better Listener." Fast Company. www.fastcompany.com/3042330/how-to-be-a-success-at-everything/how-one-simple-change-can-make-you-a-better-listener (February 13, 2015).

Chapter 9

42 McLeod, Saul. "Attachment Theory." Simple Psychology.

43 Rubin, Gretchen. *The Happiness Project*. New York: HarperCollins. 2009.

44 Rubin, Gretchen. *The Happiness Project*. New York: HarperCollins. 2009.

45 Barsade, Sigal G. "The Ripple Effect: Emotional Contagion In Groups." 2000. Yale SOM Working Paper No. OB-01. Available at SSRN: www.ssrn.com/abstract=250894

46 *The Blues Brothers*. Directed by John Landis. 1980. Universal Pictures.

47 www.sistersofmercy.org/become-a-sister/ask-a-sister/

48 www.catholic.com/quickquestions/are-nuns-female-non-ordained-members-of-the-clergy

49 www.sistersofmercy.org/become-a-sister/ask-a-sister/

50 www.mercyworld.org/foundress/index.cfm?loadref=51

51 www.sistersofmercy.org/about-us/our-history/

52 www.mercyhighered.org/memberinst.html

53 www.iup.edu/upper.aspx?id=2067

54 *The Sound of Music*. Directed by Robert Wise. 1965. Twentieth Century Fox Film.

55 www.sistersofmercy.org/about-us/our-history/

56 www.mtaloy.edu/about-mac/

57 www.sistersofmercy.org/become-a-sister/ask-a-sister/

58 Henry, Todd. *Die Empty: Unleash Your Best Work Every Day*. New York: Penguin Group, 2013.

59 This was taken from a C-Span2 broadcast of *Book TV* on July 23, 2015. It can be viewed online: www.c-span.org/video/?327279-1/robert-grenier-88-days-kandahar

Chapter 10

None.

Chapter 11

60 Disney Institute. 2001. *Be Our Guest: Perfecting the Art of Customer Service*. New York: Disney Editions, 2001.
61 *Full Metal Jacket*. Directed by Stanley Kubrick. 1987. Warner Brothers.
62 Lapchick, Richard with Juan Dominguez, Stephens Rogers, and April Johnson. "The 2014 Racial and Gender Report Card: National Football League." ww.tidesport.org/The%202014%20NFL%20 Racial%20and%20Gender%20Report%20Card.pdf (September 10, 2014).
63 Lapchick, Richard with Angelica Guiao. "The 2015 Gender Report Card: National Association of Basketball." www.tidesport. org/The%202015%20NBA%20Racial%20and%20Gender%20 Report%20Card.pdf (July 1, 2015).
64 "Martin Niemöller: 'First they came for the Socialists...'" United States Holocaust Memorial Museum www.ushmm.org/wlc/en/ article.php?ModuleId=10007392 (August 18, 2015).

Chapter 12

65 www.marykay.com/en-US/about-mary-kay/employmentmarykay/ pages/ourvalues.aspx

Chapter 13

66 www.sistersofmercy.org/become-a-sister/ask-a-sister/
67 Buffett, Mary and David Clark. *Warren Buffett's Management Secrets*. New York: Scribner, 2009.
68 O'Brien, John A. *Semisweet: An Orphan's Journey Through the School the Hersheys Built*. Lanham, Maryland: Rowman and Littlefield, 2014.
69 *Hoosiers*. Directed by David Anspaugh. 1986. Orion Pictures.

Chapter 14

70 Ellis, Linda. "The Dash." www.linda-ellis.com/the-dash-the-dash-poem-by-linda-ellis-.html (1996).

71   *Words from Catherine.* www.mercyworld.org/foundress/index.
     cfm?loadref=226.
72   *Finding Nemo.* Stanton, Andrew. 2003. Directed by Andrew Stanton
     and Lee Unkrich. Produced by Walt Disney Pictures and Pixar
     Animation Studios.
73   Carey, Benedict. "Evidence That Little Touches Do Mean So
     Much." www.nytimes.com/2010/02/23/health/23mind.html?_r=1
     (February 22, 2010).
74   Carey, Benedict. "Evidence That Little Touches Do Mean So
     Much." www.nytimes.com/2010/02/23/health/23mind.html?_r=1
     (February 22, 2010). (*For full Cal-Berkeley study: www.socrates.
     berkeley.edu/~keltner/publications/kraus.huang.keltner.2010.pdf)
75   Stachell, Leslie. *NFL Dads Dedicated to Daughters: Inspiring Personal
     Accounts of Fatherhood from the Men of the NFL.* Chicago, Illinois:
     Triumph Books, 2010.
76   Klemash, Christian. *How to Succeed in the Game of Life: 34 Interviews
     with the World's Greatest Coaches.* Kansas City: Andrews McMeel
     Publishing, 2006.

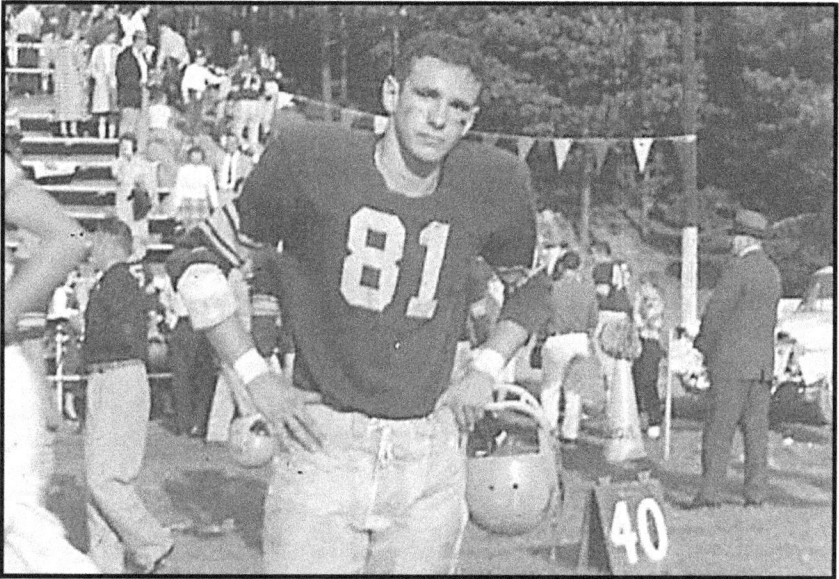

The first face on my Mount Rushmore—Jack "Iron Man" Loya—in his prime as a two-way football player in college.

The second face on my Mount Rushmore—Mike "Burt" Burton (far right)—with his team after claiming the BBL championship during the famous "Jet Wash" season.

The third face on my Mount Rushmore—Dennis Gibson—giving me instruction in a game during my Garrett days. (I'm #22...and I actually had a full head of hair back then!)

The fourth face on my Mount Rushmore—Tim Kelly—a big man with an even bigger heart, who treated everyone with respect.

The world famous Grand View Ship Hotel. It was a frequent stop for Hollywood royalty during its glory days. My bedroom was located on the top floor.

During the 1980s, my father nailed wooden planks to the building and tried to rebrand the business by renaming it Noah's Ark. Its decline is already evident in this photo.

185

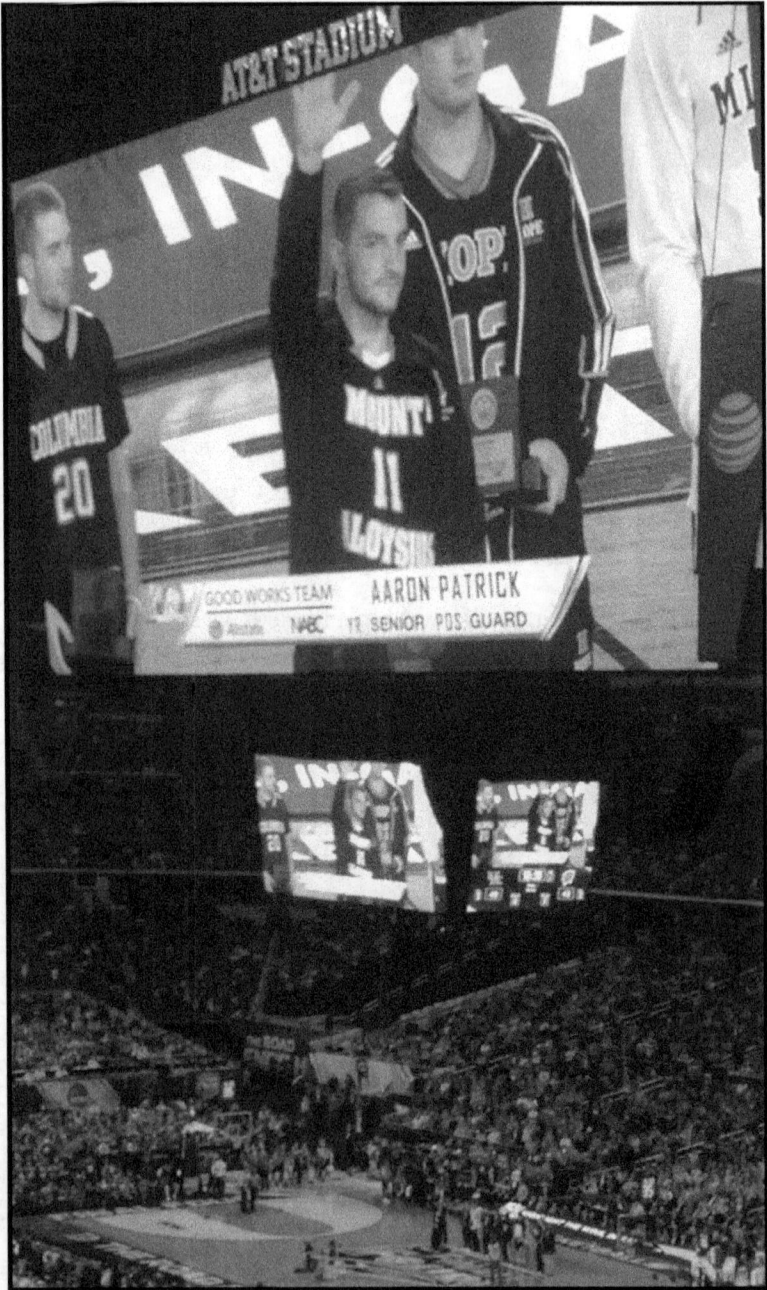

Aaron Patrick was recognized on center court at AT&T Stadium in Dallas, Texas during the 2014 NCAA Final Four. I cried when I saw him on that huge video screen.

186

Aaron Patrick poses with me moments before he walked to the court at AT&T Stadium to be recognized as a recipient of the NABC Allstate Good Works Team award.

Sister Eric Marie with me after a sports banquet. She is truly blessed... and so am I for having her in my life.

Sister Eric Marie with our team before our pre-season Mountie Madness celebration. Our players love *that* nun.

Sister Eric Marie in the locker room speaking to our players. They listen intently to every bit of advice she dispenses.

Our daughters Laken (left) and Lakota (right) give Minnie Mouse a big hug during one of our family's trips to Disney World.

A counselor talks to his team before the All Star game at my basketball camp. Notice the "Good Teammate" message printed on the back of the kids' shirts.

Be a Good Teammate

A children's book written and illustrated by Coach Lance Loya that explains the importance of being a good teammate. Everybody is part of a team in some capacity...and the world cannot have too many good teammates!

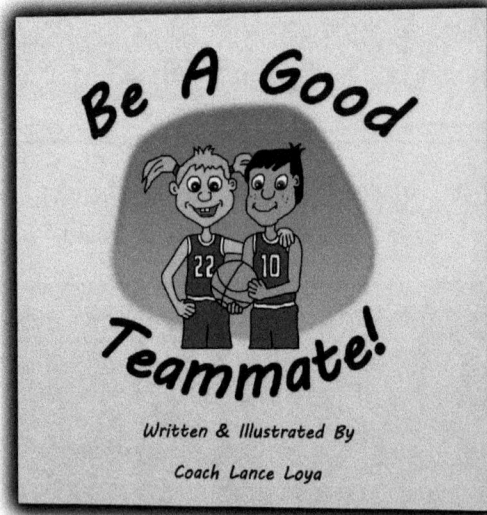

Be A Good Teammate!

Written & Illustrated By

Coach Lance Loya

Available wherever books are sold.